D1741244

Old London Gardens

1 BUCKINGHAM HOUSE from St. James's Park, *c.* 1815

From a water-colour by Copley Fielding

Old London Gardens

By

GLADYS TAYLOR

IAN HENRY PUBLICATIONS
1977

Copyright © Gladys Taylor, 1953

*First published by
B. T. Batsford, Ltd.*

This edition, 1977

*Reprinted by permission of the executors
of the late Annie Gladys Taylor*

ISBN 0 86025 806 8

 British Library Cataloguing in Publication Data

```
Taylor, Gladys
   Old London gardens.
   Bibl. - Index.
   0-86025-806-8
   1. Title
   712'.6'09421  SB451
   Gardens - England - London - History
```

*Made and printed in Great Britain by
Galliard (Printers) Ltd, Great Yarmouth, Norfolk
for Ian Henry Publications, Ltd,
38 Parkstone Avenue, Hornchurch, Essex, RM11 3LW*

CONTENTS

ACKNOWLEDGMENT

THE Author acknowledges her indebtedness to Her Majesty the Queen for permission to write about the Royal Gardens of Buckingham Palace, Kensington Palace and Kew; to His Grace the Archbishop of Canterbury, for permission to see the garden at Lambeth Palace; to His Grace the Duke of Northumberland, for permission to see the whole of the gardens at Syon House; to The Lord Bishop of London, for permission to see the gardens at Fulham Palace; to the Very Reverend the Dean of Westminster, for showing the old Infirmary Garden, and to the Librarian and Keeper of the Muniments for giving additional information; to The Master of Charterhouse, for information given; to The Masters and Benchers of Lincoln's Inn, Middle Temple, Inner Temple and Gray's Inn, for facilities and information; to the Lieutenant and Governor of the Royal Hospital, Chelsea; to the Royal Horticultural Society, for library facilities; to the Assistant Keeper of the Department of Woodwork at the Victoria and Albert Museum, for information about Ham House; to The London Gardens Society, the Women's Voluntary Services, the Director of Housing and Valuer, London County Council, for information given; to the assistants at the St. Marylebone and Hampstead Reference Libraries; and, last but not least, to the experienced and knowledgeable gardeners who have shown her round various gardens.

The extract from *The Story of Lambeth Palace* is reprinted by permission of the Author, Mrs. Dorothy Gardiner, and the Publishers, Messrs. Constable & Company, Ltd.

The Author and Publishers also wish to thank the following for permission to reproduce the illustrations in this book: the Ashmolean Museum, Oxford, for fig. 14; the Trustees of the British Museum, for figs. 1, 4 and 35; Country Life, Ltd., for fig. 21; Brinsley Ford, Esq., for fig. 43; Mr. McIntyre, Park Superintendent, Chiswick House, for the photographs of old prints of Chiswick House; the National Portrait Gallery, for figs. 26 and 27; the Governors of St. Bartholomew's Hospital, for fig. 12; the Trustees of the Victoria and Albert Museum, for fig. 28; and Messrs. Leggatt, St. James's Place, London, for figs. 30 and 31.

LIST OF ILLUSTRATIONS

LIST OF ILLUSTRATIONS

THE TAILPIECES

The vignettes at the ends of chapters are taken from the following sources: *The Gardener's Magazine of Botany* (for the tailpieces on pages 52, 121 and 160); an illustrated edition of Mary Russell Mitford's *Our Village*, 1876 (for the tailpiece by W. H. J. Boot on page 64); Thomas Bewick's *History of Quadrupeds*, 1791 (for the tailpieces on pages 58 and 186); the 1714 edition, illustrated by Lud. du Guernier, of Pope's *Rape of the Lock* (for the tailpiece on page 93); a woodcut for a Banbury Chap-Book, by John Bewick (for the tailpiece on page 77); a woodcut by Craig and Sears for an early edition of Oliver Goldsmith's *The Vicar of Wakefield* (for the tailpiece on page 104); and Humphry Repton's *Fragments on the Theory and Practice of Landscape Gardening*, 1816 (for the gardening Trophy on page 148).

CHAPTER I

The Earliest Gardens

Monastic Gardens — Westminster Abbey

THE past never dies: it only recedes into the background of the present, thereby enriching it. And sometimes it revives—as when some dim and faded tapestry is caught in a ray of sunlight, and scraps of the pattern suddenly bloom with long-forgotten colours. As we go our ways about London the names of streets and buildings remind us of what once stood in their place: the past leaps to meet us, the centuries mingle, and we are aware of continuity like a golden thread running through the tapestry of past and present and linking them together. Into that historical continuity must surely be woven gardens and memories of gardens—orchards and herb-gardens, lawns and trees, vines and flowers—whose fragrance and beauty drift across the centuries to us; for London has always been a city of gardens.

"God Almighty first planted a Garden. And indeed it is the purest of human pleasures. It is the greatest refreshment to the spirit of man; without which buildings and palaces are but gross handyworks." Thus Francis Bacon; and to those who study them, gardens reveal three aspects—horticulture, history and human interest. There are the various styles of gardening carried out at different periods of time, mediaeval, Tudor, Restoration, etc., with emphasis on the herbs and trees grown, flowers or decorative features as the case may be. There is the imprint of historical events or personages made upon some gardens—and also the reverse process—to be considered. Has anyone ever tried to estimate the influence of gardens upon history? The thought will recur in the course of this book. Undoubtedly they have played a large and important part —far greater than we shall ever realize or know, for their influence on the minds of men has mostly been subconscious.

And then there is the human interest, which is always so fascinating.

In their gardens we meet famous figures of history relaxed and at their ease, amongst their families or entertaining their friends, planning improvements with their gardeners, ordering this or that in the way of plants and seeds, overseeing the work, doing jobs themselves. We see Cardinal Wolsey walking with his chaplain and saying Vespers in his garden at Hampton Court; Pepys burying his "parmazan cheese" and wine in the garden during the Great Fire; John Evelyn planting holly hedges; Queen Mary II superintending her gardeners . . .

But we are running on too fast. Let us go back to the beginning.

*　　　*　　　*　　　*

So dim and distant is the past that we can perceive nothing of earliest London through the mists of antiquity save wattle and daub huts by the riverside. There may have been roughly cultivated patches of land: we do not know. And knowledge must be eked out with imagination as we try to reconstruct the Londinium of the Romans—a town of administrative buildings, villas, hovels and taverns, a noisy bustling town of which a model and plan can be seen in the crypt of the church of All-Hallows-by-the-Tower. The villas of the wealthy probably had gardens attached to them, laid out according to designs then fashionable at Rome: in horticulture the Romans were so far advanced that centuries elapsed before other nations caught up with them. Picture, then, beautiful formal gardens with colonnades, topiary work, terraces and alleys, fit accompaniment for tessellated pavements and elegant architecture. There would be box-edged beds of round or rectangular shape wherein the favourite flowers, violets, narcissi, roses and hyacinths bloomed; there would be fountains.

Vines were also grown by the Romans in Britain, and their cultivation, except for the gap following the departure of the invaders, continued. There are records of pre-Conquest vineyards in Somerset, Berkshire, Essex, Ware and Westminster; and about thirty-eight in different counties are mentioned in Domesday Book. Vegetables and fruit would be grown in abundance, for the rich Romans believed in good living: they thought highly of cabbage, both raw and cooked, and probably cultivated asparagus, lettuce, beet, endive, fennel and leek. When the foreign legions went away the villas fell into decay and the neglected gardens reverted to a wild state; but their owners left us a legacy of trees—box, lime, sycamore and sweet chestnut for certain, and probably mulberry, quince, peach, plum, medlar and fig as well. Of these only the very strong and well-acclimatized survived the lack of cultivation: many died out and were re-introduced later.

With the departure of the Romans the mists of antiquity gather once more round London and shroud it from our view. There succeeded the Dark Ages of the fifth and sixth centuries, of which our knowledge is so

2 A Convent Garden of 1490
From "Medieval Gardens" by Sir Frank Crisp, Bt.

slight that legend takes the place of history. When next the cloudy veils are lifted it is to disclose a Christian city of churches and monasteries—and gardens.

London after the Conquest was a city chiefly composed of churches and convents. By the time of Henry II it held 126 parish churches, each standing in its own churchyard, and thirteen religious houses with gardens and enclosures attached. There were also private gardens, some of them bursting their bounds, for "the Town Ditche without the Wall of the Citie" (finished in 1213) "was in some places altogether stopped up for gardens planted and houses builded thereon even to the very wall." Looking back we can

> ". . . dream of London, small and white and clean,
> The clear Thames bordered by its gardens green."
> (William Morris)

The most important gardens were, of course, those belonging to the conventual establishments. In their simplest form the monastic buildings were grouped round a central quadrangle which later developed into the cloister garth. From very early days this partly paved court seems to have been planted with trees and herbs. It was the most secluded part of the monastery, and in the centre there was usually a well or fountain that, besides supplying water for the needs of the house, provided a suitable spot for the monks' meditations. During times of constant warfare the cloister was the only place where rest and tranquillity could be found. How precious must that quietness have been to those who sought asylum within the monastery walls!

This garden was usually laid out in long, straight, narrow beds, and was a most necessary adjunct to the establishment, for in it were grown vegetables for the food of the monks, and simples for the healing of the sick. There were no hospitals: ailing folk came to the monasteries to be treated, or were visited in their homes by the monks. Practically all the medicines available consisted of herbs grown in the monastic gardens, such as sage, rue, southernwood and wormwood, horehound, mint, and even roses, lilies and peonies, which had a medicinal value in those days. Sometimes plants would be used in their dried state, and from this we derive our word *drug*, which is part of the Anglo-Saxon verb *drigan*, to dry. For vegetables and seasoning there would be plenty of fennel to eat with fish on fast days, as well as kale, radish, leek, onion, coriander, chervil, parsley, turnip, mallow and lovage.

It must be remembered that in early times the word *herb* had a wide significance, and really meant *plants* as distinct from trees: flowering herbs were flowering plants. Soon the monasteries had orchards, that is is to say, *wyrt geards* or *ort geards*—gardens for *wyrtan* or *orts*, names in general use for any kind of herb or vegetable. The cloister garth was originally the cloister *geard*; and our word *garden* is the plural of *geard*, and signifies a series of enclosures or plantations for various purposes, e.g. the ort-yard, the apple-yard (the fruit of which was used for cider), and the ash-yard (where the ash for hop-poles was grown). And the orchard did not contain only fruit trees: elm and oak and other forest trees were planted therein.

By degrees the enclosed central space in the monastery became known as the Infirmary garden, and for convenience' sake was placed near the infirmary or hospital. The sacristan usually had a portion of this ground or a separate plot where he grew flowers for the decoration of the church, for adorning shrines, wreathing candles and crowning the priests during processions or services. He had not a very wide choice of flowers at this time—only Madonna lilies, roses, poppies, peonies, irises and violets—but they sufficed; and, incidentally, were all used medicinally as well. On very great occasions extra flowers had to be bought, and as late as the fifteenth century churchwardens' accounts at St. Mary Hill tell of "Garlondes on Corpus Christi day, 10*d*.—A dozen and a half rose garlondes on St. Barnebe's day, 8½*d*. For two doss. di bocse garlondes for prests and clerkes on St. Barnebe daye."

Sometimes the little plot set aside was delightfully known as "Paradise." In Winchester a bricked-up doorway near one end of the cathedral still exists that led to the sacristan's garden in the ninth century, and the place is called "Paradise" to this day. Henry VI left a similar garden to the church of Eton College in his will, "for to sett in certaine trees and flowers, behovable and convenient for the service of the same church," and he ordered that it should be surrounded by "a good high wall with towers convenient thereto."

The monastery gardens in London grew in proportion with the increasing size of their buildings and number of their inhabitants. The establishments belonging to the Grey, Black, White and Austin (Augustinian) Friars had gardens within their precincts: so had the Hospitaller Orders of the Knights Templars and the Knights of St. John of Jerusalem. And the greater houses such as Westminster Abbey and the Priories of St. Martin-le-Grand, Holy Trinity, St. Bartholomew and St. Helen's had bigger enclosures.

Next in importance to the herb garden were the orchard and the vineyard. Orchards were planted with apples for eating, cooking and making cider; and with pears, cherries and quinces: the wine from the vineyards was variable in quality. There were also dovecotes, and fish-ponds containing pike, perch, carp, bream and trout. These ponds had at one end a small tank known as the "stew," where the fish already netted were kept till needed. Some monasteries boasted a "coney garth," or rabbit enclosure. This was helpful because it supplied fresh meat during the winter. Cattle had to be killed in autumn because there was no winter fodder for them, and the carcases, salted down, provided a somewhat monotonous diet from which rabbit flesh afforded a welcome change. All this produce was necessary for the upkeep of the monasteries: not only did it provide food for the inhabitants, but any surplus was sold to bring in revenue.

Westminster Abbey can be taken as a typical example of a large monastic establishment, and as we wander in the neighbourhood we can try to reconstruct the past. Thorney Island, or the Isle of Thorns, was created by branches of the "Tye burn," which, rising in Hampstead, divided into two when it reached St. James's Park. These streams were known as the Long Ditch and the Mill Ditch, and they both flowed into the Thames. At high water Thorney was probably completely insulated. The Long Ditch followed the direction of Storey's Gate and Great George Street, and emptied itself into the Thames near Westminster Bridge: the Mill Ditch turned south and followed the line of Prince's Street, Great Smith Street, Great College Street, and so into the Thames at Millbank near the Victoria Tower. On the land thus enclosed rose West-monastery with its church dedicated to St. Peter. The King's Palace of Westminster was built between the monastery and the river.

The property of this Benedictine establishment was extensive, and stretched from Millbank to Covent Garden, from the Thames to Hyde Park. With all these wide lands Westminster remained a delightfully rural spot right up to the Dissolution: a document of Henry VIII's time refers to its "houses, barnes, stables, dove-houses, orchards, gardens, pools, fisheries, waters, ditches, lands, meadows and pastures." These were all essential to the maintenance of the establishment, for the monks formed only a fraction of the inhabitants of the Abbey; the brethren probably never exceeded fifty in number. But a monastery of this size and importance was like a village, and would have school-boys, pensioners, choir, secretaries, servants, masons, plumbers and carpenters to the number of about 350—as well as a constant stream of pilgrims to be fed. There was, however, one class of people for whom food had not to be provided, i.e. those who took sanctuary within the Abbey precincts. Sanctuary, in the Middle Ages, meant physical safety and nothing more; sustenance was not included; and many poor wretches who had neither relatives nor friends to bring them food actually died of starvation while taking refuge from their enemies.

As may be imagined, there were many enclosures within the precincts of Westminster Abbey; but although their names have come down to us, their positions are sometimes difficult to locate. The site of Abbey Orchard Street is obvious: here the monks had their orchard of trees from which, in 1362, the Infirmarer, John de Morden, obtained 9s. for his apples, and the following year 10s. (a goodly sum in those days) for pears and apples. Until fairly recent times Bowling Street and Vine Street used to mark respectively where the bowling alley and the vineyard lay. The vineyard was still doing well in 1618, when, according to the Issue Rolls of Exchequer in James I's reign, fish-ponds were made in the "vine garden" "for the King's cormorants, ospreys and otters."

The Mill Ditch, where it joined the Thames, turned the Abbot's mill at Millbank. Market Street, till lately, ran where formerly the "Market Mede" or market garden was situated. On the west of the monastery buildings was the granary, a long building with a tower, that was supported on arches; and near it stood the oxstall, or stall for cattle, and the barn. The former farmyard with its poultry is now Dean's Yard.

Various officials were entitled to private gardens of their own. West of the infirmary and its garden stretched the "Grete" garden. The Abbot's garden lay in part of what is now Broad Sanctuary, in the north-west angle of the old wall. Beyond the Mill Ditch were "Precentor's Mede" or "Chaunter's Hull" (which explains itself, as does "Almoner's Mede" or "Almery" garden), and the "Hostry" garden on the site of St. John's church. The "conyn garth" or rabbit enclosure was in "Maudit's" garden (named after an Earl of Warwick who exchanged some land with the Abbey). This garden or "toft" was also known as "Caley's" (a corruption of "Calais") because of the wool staplers of Calais who came to live near—just as Petty France was named after the French merchants there.

Water for the monastery was conveyed in leaden pipes from springs in the manor of Hyde (now Hyde Park), which belonged to the monks until the Dissolution. To-day a stone monument standing above the Dell north-east of the bridge across the Serpentine, bears this inscription:

"A supply of water by conduit from this spot was granted to the Abbey of Westminster with the manor of Hyde by King Edward the Confessor. The manor was resumed by the Crown in 1536 but the springs as a head and original fountain of water were preserved to the Abbey by the charter of Queen Elizabeth in 1560."

The Cellarer had a large garden farther away—the Convent (or, in Norman-French, "couvent") garden, which is Covent Garden to-day; and close by lay the pastures of Long Acre. On the site of St. Martin-in-the-Fields stood a little chapel where the black-robed monks labouring in that part of the grounds might go to pray. As Benedictines, work on the land was enjoined by the Rule of their Order; and it is to these monks especially that the science of horticulture owed so much in the Middle Ages. They cultivated plants and learned their uses, and spread the knowledge abroad.

To-day we can only partly reconstruct these great possessions with the aid of imagination. Yet one small intimate spot has survived from the ninth century—that is, from before the Confessor's time. Hidden away in the heart of the old Abbey lies the garden of the infirmary, now known as College Garden (3). It is a quiet quadrangle of lawns and gravelled paths and plane trees. The ancient boundary wall, built in 1374–5, still exists in part between the surrounding buildings, and on one side three Norman arches and their supporting pillars—practically all that is left of the chapel of St. Katherine—are embedded in a later wall.

From the lawns one looks up to the fourteenth-century square stone bulk of the Jewel Tower, and, beyond, the western towers of the great historic Abbey rising into the sky. So much has happened in the world outside this secluded garden during the thousand years of its existence: there have been conquest and changes of dynasty, rebellions, treason and plots, religious intolerance and persecution, plague and fire, coronations, weddings and funerals, political changes, war in the air—and yet "among all the changes and chances of this mortal life" the little plot has lain quiet and serene, a refuge from trouble and disturbance. The peace of centuries is distilled and held here.

This herb garden was a vital part of the monastery, as in the plot were

18

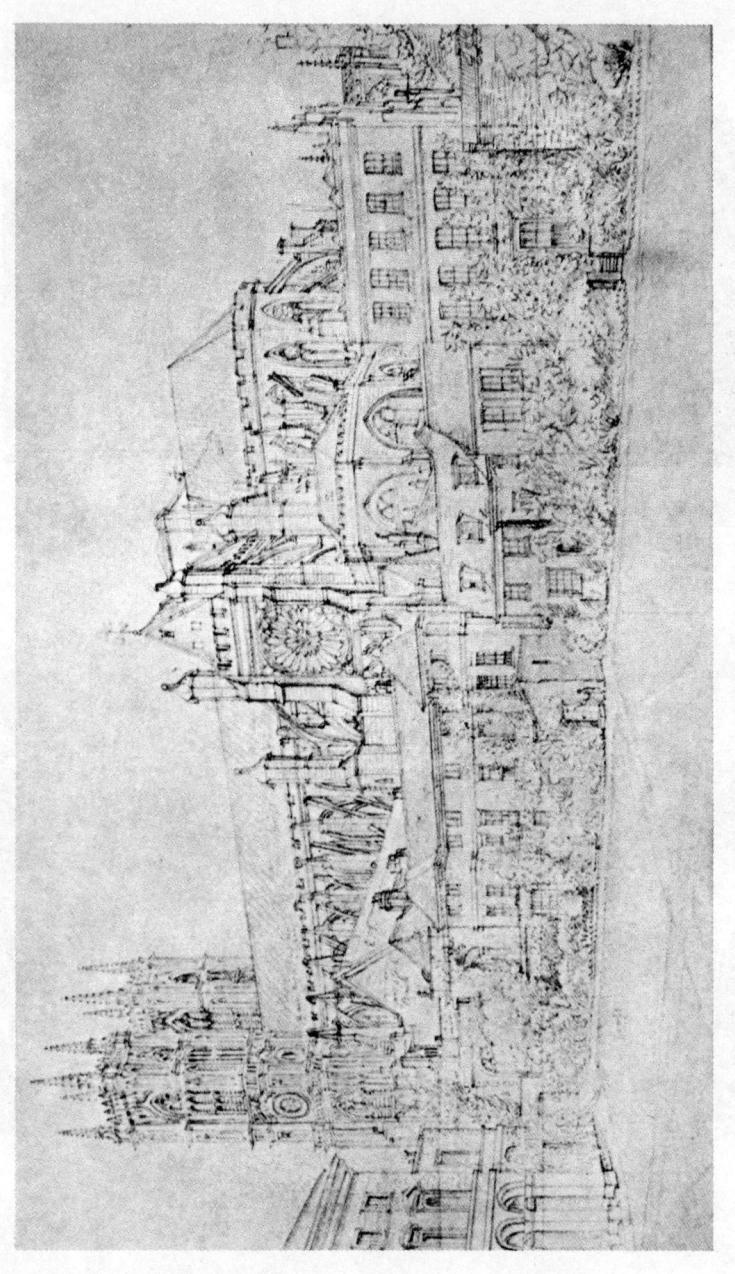

3   WESTMINSTER ABBEY: College Garden, formerly the Infirmary Garden, with houses on the north side
From a drawing by William Capon, 1819

4   ELY PLACE: A south view, about 1780
From a water-colour by Francis Grose

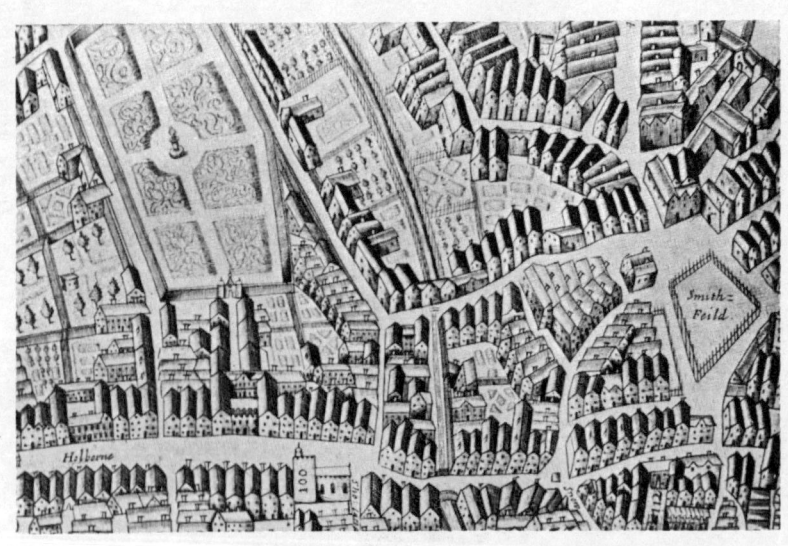

5   ELY PLACE (top left) in 1658
Detail of a map by Faithorne

grown the necessary plants of healing for the sick brethren. The Infirmarer supervised the concoction of homely medicines, and the Abbey Rolls record the purchase of honey for syrups, and payments for ginger, licorice, "popeye," camomile, etc. Even lily roots figured in the accounts: threepence was spent on their purchase in 1320–1—but we are not told for what medicinal purpose they were used.

There was a pond in the garden, and also a dovecote: in 1369–70 a new Columbary was built at a cost of £8. The Infirmarer had heavy expenses to meet in the care of the sick and aged monks, and he made money in whatever ways he could. Osiers from a bed at the junction of the Mill Ditch and the Thames usually yielded about 10s. a year; the sale of pears and apples brought him profit, as we have already seen, but the dovecote was a perpetual disappointment as a source of income. Year after year occurs this plaintive entry in the Account Rolls: "From the Dovecot this year—nothing."

The little enclosure, one acre in extent, was the pleasure garden of the sick monks. Here they took their recreation, pacing along the paths between the narrow beds of herbs and under the fruit trees. Later there seems to have been more active exercise in the garden, for in 1462 a space was cleared "pro les buttes" (archery butts), and in 1468 "turfes pro lez buttes et les herbes" were bought. A postern gate in the wall communicated with the adjacent grounds of Westminster Palace, and one can imagine that the monks did not find this an unmixed blessing.

On the north of the garden extended the chapel of St. Katherine, the infirmary chapel, which was probably built in the middle of the twelfth century. This was quite a large building, having a quire 24½ ft. long internally, and a nave of five equal bays of 9 ft. 5 in. with aisles on either side. Many consecrations of bishops (including St. Hugh of Lincoln and William of Worcester) took place there before the Reformation, and also important councils. At one of these, in 1176, the chapel was the scene of a most unseemly brawl between the Archbishops of Canterbury and York when a question of precedence arose. Which of them was entitled to sit on the presiding Cardinal's right hand? York took the place of honour, whereupon Canterbury sat in his lap. Then the archepiscopal servants rushed to the defence of their respective masters and began fighting. The Cardinal fled, the assembly broke up in confusion—and the vexed question of precedence was finally settled by the Pope. It seems strange that such an historic church should be deliberately destroyed by order; but that was its fate in Elizabeth's reign.

In Benedictine monasteries it was usual for the infirmary hall to adjoin the chapel so that sick monks and the aged, who had permanent quarters in the infirmary, could join in the services. This arrangement can be seen in the ruins of the infirmary at Canterbury, and Westminster was no exception to the rule. The infirmary hall stood on the site of the present Little Cloisters; and as the hall opened into the garden as well, the brethren could worship and also watch the annual recurring miracle of spring blossoms outside and listen to the bird-song, while those who could hobble about sat in the sunshine among flowers and sweet-smelling herbs. Then, as now, the garden was a place of peace and of healing for mind as well as body.

This enclosure (or was it Dean's Yard, as some assert?) appears in history on one more occasion. In 1540 the Abbey of Westminster was quietly dissolved; but the Benedictines, under Abbot Feckenham, returned in Mary's reign. After her death the monastery finally passed out of their hands; and Fuller, the historian, thus describes the closing scene:

"Queen Elizabeth coming to the crown, sent for abbot Feckenham to come to her, whom the messenger found setting of elms in the orchard" (College Garden or Dean's Yard) "of Westminster Abbey. But he would not follow the messenger till first he had finished his plantation. . . . Coming afterwards to the queen, what discourse passed between them they themselves know alone. Some have confidently guessed she proffered him the archbishopric of Canterbury on condition he would conform to her laws, which he utterly refused."

Feckenham ended his days in prison, and his Abbey was shortly afterwards made into a College; but his elms survived as a row of trees till 1779. They were then cut down.

CHAPTER II

Mediaeval Gardens

Ely Place — The Inns of Court

TWO famous gardens belong to the thirteenth century: one was owned by the Bishops of Ely, the other by Henry de Lacy, Earl of Lincoln, and they were both situated in Holborn, which was at that time a completely rural spot outside the City.

To-day Ely Place consists of two rows of very ordinary houses and a small, ancient church that with the passing of centuries and the accumulation of dust and mud and rubbish on the surface of the ground is now sunk below the level of the roadway. At a first glance the scene appears dull and commonplace, but to those who can look behind the present to the past it is full of romance and interest that go back nearly 700 years. Here, on the site of the present Ely Place and its near-by houses, streets and alleys stood the town house of the Bishops of Ely with its immense gardens (9, 5). Beginning in 1290 as "a messuage" (dwelling-place and adjoining garden) "and 9 cottages in Holbourne," it became one of the most magnificent houses in London, with a meadow, kitchen garden, orchard and vineyard. The old chapel of the Bishops, St. Ethelreda, also belongs to the thirteenth century.

The earliest records of the garden are still preserved at Ely. They date from Edward III's reign, and mention names of neighbouring houses and streets that are recognizable, such as "Faryndonesin" (Faringdon's Inn). The grounds lay north of the mansion, and were enclosed by a thorn hedge in which were wooden gates fitted with locks and keys. Four cartloads of thorns were bought and used for making this hedge, and the cost of the thorns was 6s. 8d. Inner gardens were reserved for the Bishops' private use; and railings and locked doors separated the great garden and the "grass-yard" or meadow from the vineyard. Every year the "grass-yard" was mown, and the grass or hay sold, a tithe of the proceeds being paid to the Rector of St. Andrew's,

Holborn. Other sales in 1372-3, which may be taken as a typical year, were of onions and garlick, beans in the husk, herbs, "lekes," parsley and herbage.

Our present Vine Street commemorates the site of the vineyard. Holborn seems to have been a favourite locality for grapes: close to Ely Place was the vineyard belonging to the Earl of Lincoln, and not far off, in Smithfield, another owned by the Canons of Trinity Church. Viticulture, already flourishing in England at the time of the Norman Conquest, received a further stimulus with the advent of foreign priors and abbots from vine-growing countries, who introduced improvements in the vineyards, and new kinds of grapes. The episcopal vineyard at Ely Place was evidently troublesome, and for many years it was let. In spite of engaging extra "labourers and women" and a boy for digging, dressing and weeding it, the wine produced was so sour as to be more like vinegar, and 30 gallons of "verjuice" were made one year.

In Elizabeth's reign the garden was famous for its strawberries, and we find Shakespeare referring to them in *Richard III*:

> *Duke of Gloster.* My lord of Ely, when I was last in Holborn
> I saw good strawberries in your garden there;
> I do beseech you, send for some of them!
> *Ely.* Marry, I will, my lord, with all my heart.

During this same reign the Bishop of Ely, Dr. Cox, one of the earliest reformers, was subjected to humiliation at the hands of the Queen. Sir Christopher Hatton so beguiled her Majesty that she made him Chancellor, and allowed him to settle down comfortably in part of Ely Place. He took most of the gatehouse as his residence and also held a portion of the garden on a lease of twenty-one years at the nominal rent of a red rose for the gatehouse, ten loads of hay and £10 per annum for the garden. The poor Bishop was only allowed the right of passing through the gatehouse, of walking in his own garden, and of gathering 20 bushels of roses every year. Hatton begged the Queen to let him have the whole of the property—at which the Bishop protested strongly, but without any effect. However, retribution overtook Elizabeth's "dancing Chancellor." The Queen, who could be a hard bargain-driver if she chose, later demanded repayment of the huge sums she had lent him; and this so crushed Hatton that, being unable to meet those debts, he died of a broken heart, owing the Crown £40,000. His memory is perpetuated in Hatton Garden, the street of diamond merchants, that runs almost parallel with Ely Place at the back of St. Ethelreda's church.

Twenty bushels of roses! One wonders how they were measured—whether by weight or capacity. Did the Bishop sacrifice the beauty of long leafy sprays for the sake of getting as many short-stemmed blooms as possible? And what different kinds did he gather?

Roses were the chief flowers in the garden, and the favourite was the sweet-scented double red *Rosa gallica*: this was the red rose of England, which has flourished here from time immemorial. The white rose of England, *Rosa alba*, is equally ancient, and would also have been found in the Bishop's garden in company with the fragrant old cabbage rose, the Red Provence (*Rosa centifolia*), which was introduced by the Romans. Other varieties grown in Elizabeth's reign included damask roses (*Rosa damascena*) probably brought from the gardens of Damascus by the Crusaders: their deep pink petals, golden hearts and delicious scent made them a favourite kind for centuries. Happily, in our own day varieties of this rose are still grown, their colours ranging from white to red. *Rosa mundi*, with striped red and white petals, is another very old rose, and has been associated with Fair Rosamund of the twelfth century, and also with the union of the red and white roses of England; however, the true York and Lancaster rose, a variety of damask, is not striped but white with an occasional red petal.

Quite "modern" roses at Ely Place would be the musk rose (*Rosa moschata*) mentioned by Shakespeare (though his eglantine sweet-briar had been known for hundreds of years) and the cinnamon rose (*Rosa cinnamomea*) with large flat pink flowers. Possibly there were delicate yellow Provence roses (*Rosa sulphurea*); but in any case the Bishop's 20 bushels would include a good many kinds—all of them sweetly scented—which is more than can be said of our present-day sophisticated beauties! And how they must have soothed his wounded spirit.

One wonders about the later history of such a notable estate. What happened eventually to the famous garden?

During the years 1620–4 Ely Place was occupied by the Spanish Embassy; between 1640 and 1660 most of the property disappeared. The grounds must have been built over, for we are told that only the chapel and the hall remained. So passed away a garden that had been celebrated for nearly 300 years.

*   *   *   *

Not far from Ely Place stood another famous house and garden, belonging to Henry de Lacy, Earl of Lincoln. Originally this had been the monastery of the Dominicans when they came to England first in 1221. But after fifty-five years the black-robed monks were able to build a new House (Blackfriars) for themselves on the bank of the river Fleet, outside the City wall, and Edward I then granted their former estate to the Earl of Lincoln in 1286.

This nobleman had many manors and gardens in various parts of the country, but that in Holborn was the most productive—possibly as a result of its previous cultivation by the monks. The garden stretched down to the stream, and was enclosed by wooden palings. Many kinds of flowers were grown there; not only roses but Madonna lilies, lavender, clove pinks and thyme as well as peonies, irises of purple, white and yellow, honeysuckle, hollyhocks and corncockles. A fish stew known as the "greater ditch" contained pike that were fed artificially; and the orchard yielded many kinds of apples, pears, cherries and nuts. Imagine all these growing in Holborn!

Any surplus produce was marketed; and the accounts tell of the sale of "herbage of the garden" (hay), "hemp of the garden," onions, garlick and "little plantes." One year 8s. 0½d. was spent on the purchase of eels, small fish and small frogs "for the sustenance of the pike." Besides the fish stew there was a coney garth well stocked with game of every kind in addition to rabbits, and a vineyard—all dating from the time of the Dominicans. The grapes, however, cannot have been very sweet, for in one year 49 gallons of verjuice were made from them.

The Earl was keenly interested in his gardens, and made a practice of obtaining slips of new pears and apples from the Continent to enrich his orchards. From this time dates the costard apple which was popular for many centuries, and which gave its name to costermongers, i.e. "mongers" or sellers of costards. Another apple that goes back thus far is the pearmain: this was used for making cider.

In accordance with the custom of those days his lordship's residence became known as his "Inn" or town house: what we call an inn was then a tavern. It is said, but not reliably, that in 1310 he began to take law students into his house: what is certain is that in 1350 the present Society occupied buildings known as Lyncolnesynne, which they rented from Thomas de Lincoln, King's Serjeant of Holborn. Between 1412 and 1422 they moved to a site close to the present Old Hall; and

Lincoln's Inn gardens are actually situated on part of the Earl's famous garden. His elaborate crest of fifteen mill-irons and a rampant lion forms the crest of the Inn, and can be seen over the gateway into Chancery ("Chancellor") Lane and in many other places. More land was acquired from the neighbouring property of the Bishop of Chichester (still remembered in Chichester Rents and Bishop's Court near-by). And a plot of ground comprising a garden and a coney garth was rented from one William Cottrell, and was sometimes referred to as "Cottrell's Garden."

The coney garth held all kinds of game, and various penalties were enforced from the time of Edward IV to Henry VIII on students who shot at rabbits with bows and arrows. But in 1572 permission was given to the students to shoot two rabbits a night in the coney garth "for ever after," to vary and improve their food in hall. At one time a wall (where the 1914–19 War Memorial stands) divided the upper garden from the lower where the rabbits were kept, but when the coney garth was done away with a wall was no longer needed, and that enclosure is now New Square. The wild duck that frequent the lily pond are the only reminder of the game that was once preserved there.

The garden in 1558 was separated from Ficket's Field, "an adjacent meadow" (Lincoln's Inn Fields), by a clay embankment. Later this was replaced by a brick wall with a gate that is probably the same as the little postern north of the new hall to-day. But the garden ran farther along the wall then, and covered the ground where the new hall and library stand: they were only built in 1845. The terrace against the wall was made in 1663, and during that summer Pepys came with his wife "to Lincolne's Inne, and there walked up and down to see the new garden which they are making, and will be very pretty" (6). When completed they must have been attractive, for in 1765 a foreigner visiting London noted that "The grass plots of the gardens at Lincoln's Inn are adorned with statues, which, taken all together, form a scene very pleasing to the eye."

The statues have vanished, but the sundial with its inscription, *Qua redit nescitis horam*, which was set up in 1794 during William Pitt's Treasurership, still survives in spite of the bombing that damaged New Square, Old Buildings and Stone Buildings in the last war.

Like the other Inns of Court, Lincoln's Inn Walks have been a place of fashionable resort in the past. To-day the gardens are private, but by the courtesy of the Master of the Benchers are open from 12.0 to 2.30, Mondays to Fridays, "for the enjoyment of rest and quiet." And so we can sit among flowers on the terrace, with pigeons strolling at our feet, or walk along the shady avenue in the garden and muse on the past.

Across the road lie Lincoln's Inn Fields, looking so peaceful that it is difficult to imagine them as they were—"a wild-looking place of evil repute, and the scene of bloody executions." Deeds of violence were common, and it will be remembered that Lord William Russell was executed here in 1683 on the charge of being concerned in the Rye House Plot. During the early part of the eighteenth century the Fields, lying waste and piled with rubbish, were the haunt of all kinds of worthless characters—thieves, vagrants, "mumpers, rufflers" and even cripples—who used to intimidate passers-by. Now the scene is entirely changed: the notorious Fields are as prettily laid out as any of the London Squares, and are a welcome refuge from the noise of Holborn. Their former rustic situation is brought to mind by Great Turnstile Street and Little Turnstile Street.

*   *   *   *

The gardens of the Temple, one of the most dignified and reposeful spots in London, go back to 1185, when the proud and zealous brotherhood of the Knights Templars, "The Order of the Poor Fellow-Soldiers of Jesus Christ," moved from their original quarters in Holborn, and built a huge monastery by the riverside. It stood practically in open country, for next on the west was the Bishop of Exeter's house and garden, then came the Savoy Palace on the river front, and beyond that a few houses, and meadows with streams. The grounds of the Temple, sloping down to the Thames, were smaller than at present, for the river was not confined by any embankment but flowed wide and shallow on its course, encroaching considerably on the land at high tide. It was the main thoroughfare for traffic, and at the bottom of the Temple gardens, where trees grew along the riverside, a sort of wooden pier on arches ran out across the mud to make the landing stage of Temple Stairs.

This is not the place to give a history of the Order of soldier-monks and its gradual downfall, nor of the organized collegiate body of students and professors of common law which took over the buildings after Pope Clement V formally abolished the Knights Templars in 1312.

The Prospect of Lincoln's Inn.

6 "The Prospect of LINCOLN'S INN," 1755
From an engraving for Stow's Survey

7   THE TEMPLE as it was in 1720
After a contemporary engraving

After the suppression the monastery passed to Aimer de Valence, Earl of Pembroke, and in 1324 was given to the Knights of St. John. But they already had their own establishment in Clerkenwell, and so they granted the Temple "to the Students of the Common Lawes of England: in whose possession the same hath sithence remained." The property included not only all the consecrated ground and all that lay within the City, but some land outside the City, known as the Outer Temple. Part of this was later covered by Essex House and its celebrated garden. The separation of the Temple into Inner and Middle took place in the reign of Henry VI.

All through the centuries the gardens have been loved and cared for. Traditionally they were famous for their roses—the Old Provence, the Cabbage and the Maiden's Blush. There seems to be little historical foundation for this renown, although entries in the accounts of the Inner Temple show payments to the gardener from time to time for wire "to naile up the Rose trees in the garden." But in Chaucer's time roses were prolific in England, so what more likely than that they should be found in all their scented beauty at the Temple? Shakespeare must have known of the roses in these gardens when, in *Henry VI*, Part I, he staged there the dispute between Richard Plantagenet, Duke of York, and the Earls of Somerset, Suffolk and Warwick that led to the Wars of the Roses.

> *Plantagenet.* Since you are tongue-tied and so loth to speak,
> In dumb significants proclaim your thoughts:
> Let him that is a true-born gentleman,
> And stands upon the honour of his birth,
> If he suppose that I have pleaded truth,
> From off this brier pluck a white rose with me.
> *Somerset.* Let him that is no coward nor no flatterer
> But dare maintain the party of the truth,
> Pluck a red rose from off this thorn with me.

After Warwick, and Vernon and the lawyer present, had plucked white roses, and Suffolk a red rose, Plantagenet continued:

> Now, Somerset, where is your argument?
> *Somerset.* Here, in my scabbard, meditating that
> Shall dye your white rose in a bloody red.
> *Plantagenet.* Hath not thy rose a canker, Somerset?
> *Somerset.* Hath not thy rose a thorn, Plantagenet?

Plantagenet. Ay, sharp and piercing, to maintain his truth;
Whiles thy consuming canker eats his falsehood.
Somerset. Well, I'll find friends to wear my bleeding roses,
That shall maintain what I have said is true,
Where false Plantagenet dare not be seen.

The quarrel went on until finally Warwick prophesied:

"This brawl today,
Grown to this faction in the Temple-garden,
Shall send, between the red rose and the white,
A thousand souls to death and deadly night.

After the separation into Inner Temple and Middle Temple, the garden of the Inner Temple was in the fifteenth and sixteenth centuries divided into several enclosures. The Great Garden extended to the Thames (where in 1528 a wall was built to keep out the water) and was partly bounded on two sides by houses that had doors opening into the garden. Another enclosure was known as "le Nutgardyne," yet another as "Nuttrey Court," and a fourth as "le Olyvaunte": this was perhaps "Elephant," from a sign painted to distinguish a house facing it. A brick wall was built in 1533 to enclose two sides of the Great Garden, and for some extraordinary reason posts bearing the twelve signs of the Zodiac were set up. With the erection of houses on the site of the present Paper Buildings, the Great Garden was divided into two, and the eastern part (now King's Bench Walk) was called Benchers' Walk, and was planted with trees in formal rows.

The accounts during James I's reign show the work that was done in the garden. Posts and rails were frequently painted, trees were constantly bought, a fig tree was purchased (perhaps for Fig Tree Court), and a mulberry planted in Tanfield Court. In 1605 seats were placed "about the trees in Hare's Court": the courts must have been like little gardens at this time. A sundial placed in the garden in 1615 cost 15*s.*, and a new stone roller in an iron frame £1 9*s.* 6*d.* A pond was excavated and enclosed by railings, a new pump set up, a summer-house built with a tiled floor, and new seats made for the garden.

Care was taken of the gardens during the Commonwealth, but with the Restoration came a period of neglect. Then, with the influx of Dutch ideas in the reign of William and Mary, the gardens were transformed—and this was probably their prettiest period. A piece of ground between the King's Bench Office and Serjeants' Inn was converted into the "benchers' garden" or privy garden, and each bencher was given a key to it. Chestnuts and limes were planted, walks and grass plots laid down; bulbs were set in the ground, and orange trees in tubs. In the centre of the garden a remarkable fountain was constructed: it consisted of an artificial cherry tree made of copper, and beneath its spreading branches, a lion's face, and a copper scallop shell to hold the water. This fountain seems to have been difficult to keep in order, and was probably one of those complicated and ingenious "waterworks" in which the water could be secretly turned on to spurt out suddenly and give unwary spectators a shower-bath, or to drop its spray in an unusual way, or set machinery in motion. Such fanciful notions were extremely popular, and some fountains were even contrived to play tunes.

Many changes were made in the Great Garden. To begin with, the walks were newly laid with cockle-shells. This was a fashion of the day that also prevailed in St. James's Park, where a "Cockle-strewer" was appointed to look after the shell walks. At the Inner Temple jessamine was now grown, and the accounts mention "nails and list for the jessamy wall." Nectrons (nectarines), peaches, cherry and plum trees were planted as well as standard laurels, hollies, juniper and box trees which were probably clipped into formal shapes. The terrace already existed, and along its length were set orange trees in tubs. Until a glass-covered shed was erected in 1705 these trees were taken to nursery gardens at Islington each winter, and returned to the Temple for the summer. An entry in the accounts for 1702–3 shows expenditure

"for 6 elm trees in the walks in the room of some that were broke down, for 15 yew trees in the great garden in pots, for a yew tree in the bench garden, for 200 'junquiles' at 6s. a 100, for 200 tulips at 5s. a hundred, for 100 yellow Dutch crocus, for 50 'Armathalagum,' for 4 box trees for the grass plots, for 12 striped 'fillerayes,' etc. £8.1.0."

It seems good value for the money of those days, though nobody is quite sure what was meant by "Armathalagums": they may have been Ornithogalum, the Star of Bethlehem. "Striped 'fillerayes'" were of course variegated phillyreas which were used for topiary work. Later there are other records of 14 standard almond trees being bought, as well as 20 standard laurels, 6 junipers, 4 hollies, etc. A sundial on the steps of the Great Garden was set up for £25 by Edward Strong, the contractor and builder, under Wren, of St. Paul's cathedral.

What a delightful picture of the garden on a fine spring morning in Queen Anne's reign is conjured up by these lists of purchases! Crocuses, jonquils and tulips stand in gay but formal ranks along the flower-beds framed in green turf and separated by walks. Almond blossom might be over, but the other fruit trees would be clotted with blossom, and the clipped trees ranged primly in their decorative pots along the terrace and walks. Sunshine would bring out the warm red of the walls where rose stems and climbing jessamine were nailed; it would light to brilliance the colours of flowers and grass, and cast a deep shadow on the surface of the sundial. Budding elms would spread a hazy network of twigs and branches against the sky; and everywhere the birds would be singing (7).

In 1730 the beautiful wrought-iron gates were erected; and luckily these were not damaged in the heavy bombing that the Temple sustained during the last war. The design shows the Gray's Inn coat of arms—a griffin—as well as the Pegasus of the Inner Temple. The reason for this we shall learn when we come to Gray's Inn. Eighteenth-century accounts deal chiefly with bills for miscellaneous trees, levelling and gravelling the walks, turfing, painting the railings and seats. In 1786-7 "Mr. Elliott gardener, for his wife's keeping the seats in the garden clean" was paid £2 2s.

Sundials were fairly numerous at the Temple during the seventeenth and eighteenth centuries, but many of them no longer exist. We can still see Edward Strong's dial on its graceful, fluted plinth of stone just inside the Inner Temple's garden gates: the gnomon which casts the shadow bears the Pegasus and the letters $_R^T{}_P$ in an open design, "T" standing for Treasurer, and "R P" being the initials of the Treasurer at that time. The garden possesses another sundial, in this case upheld by the kneeling figure of a blackamoor. It was brought from Clement's Inn (which belonged to the Inner Temple) after its disestablishment in 1884. The kneeling negro was a favourite design among the makers of leaden statues in the eighteenth century, and several similar examples are known to exist. The Black Boy of the Inner Temple was probably made by a Dutch sculptor, Jan van Nost, who came to London in the reign of William III, and set up a studio in Piccadilly. A third sundial, dated 1686, survives high up on the wall of Pump Court. Instead of watching over a peaceful enclosed courtyard it now looks across a scene of devastation and ruin that makes its message strangely poignant: "SHADOWS WE ARE AND LIKE SHADOWS DEPART."

Not much information is available with regard to the gardens of the Middle Temple. For one thing, they are smaller than those of the Inner Temple, and for another, they were probably laid out in a similar fashion with the same kinds of trees and plants: old prints show this to have been the case at certain periods.

That interest was taken in the gardens can be deduced from an entry in the records for November 23rd, 1649: "Petition of one hundred and eleven gentlemen for collection to be made on a Roll towards beautifying the Garden enclosed with a new brick wall is 'denied.' Their Masterships have allowed £50, but will not be at any further charge." But possibly the gentlemen had been too exigent before. When the Treasury had granted £100 for the building of this wall the gentlemen asked for more money. Ten pounds was granted, "but time will be taken to consider to what issue this great charge will succeed." Their Masterships were canny and cautious, and were taking no chances.

The most famous spot remaining is Fountain Court. At one time this formed part of the Middle Temple Benchers' garden which also covered the ground where Garden Court stands. South of the fountain a terrace and steps stretched across to the wall of Essex House next door. Beyond the old Hall that was opened by Queen Elizabeth, and where *Twelfth Night* was played in Shakespeare's time, the rest of the garden, shady and green, ran down to the river. At high tide this lower part used to be submerged, but the embanking of the Thames at two different periods has done away with that unpleasantness, and has also enlarged the garden.

Fountain Court is a quiet spot of trees and flagstones. The fountain was originally constructed in 1681, and was greatly admired for the way in which the water was forced "to a vast and almost incredible altitude." Needless to say, it has undergone changes and been considerably modernized since that date. Charles Lamb, who was born in the Temple, loved it when a child, and used to turn the water off and on to astonish his playfellows. Many who have never seen it will be familiar with Dickens' happy description in *Martin Chuzzlewit*, where Ruth Pinch is walking in the Court with John Westlock: "Brilliantly the Temple Fountain splashed in the sun, and laughingly its liquid music played, and merrily the idle drops of water danced and danced, and peeping out in sport among the trees, plunged lightly down to hide themselves, as little Ruth and her companion came towards it."

The old seventeenth-century sundials and their Latin mottoes have vanished from the courts, but a pedestal sundial of 1719 remains at the lower end of the garden. A fairly recent addition to the gardens is the stone figure of a boy clasping a book, which stands on the lawn. This was erected in 1930 in memory of Charles Lamb, and on an open page of the book are inscribed words from his essay on *Old Benchers of the Middle Temple*: "Lawyers were children once."

Figs still flourish in the Temple gardens, and jessamine grows abundantly; there are still lawns and gravelled walks and shady trees. It is still possible to leave the noisy twentieth century behind in Fleet Street, and in a few paces find oneself in the quiet remote world of Johnson and Goldsmith, who used to sit and talk beneath a sycamore; of Lamb and his Old Benchers; of Thackeray and Dickens. Or we can slip farther back through the centuries to the arrogant white-mantled Templars who strode through the courts and across the lawns of their once-great monastery. Their emblem of the Paschal Lamb and Flag, sculptured and painted above doorways and on gate-posts in the Middle Temple brings them close to us; and the river, flowing endlessly past the garden like Time itself, reminds us that past and present are really one.

Gray's Inn also began as a private estate. The property was originally the manor of Portpool or Purpoole belonging to the Lords de Grey of Wilton, and was charmingly described in 1308 as "a messuage with gardens and one dove house and a windmill"—and a "chauntry." Its subsequent history is rather hazy; but records of the Society of Gray's Inn commence in 1569, and the crest of the de Greys—a griffin—is the crest of the Inn.

From very early times Gray's Inn Fields were used as grounds for archery and all kinds of open-air sport; and in Mary's reign Henry, Lord Berkeley, used to hunt there and towards Islington and Heygate daily with his hounds and a large company of followers, including "many gentlemen of the Innes of Court and others of lower condition . . . and 150 servants in livery that daily attended him in their tawny coats." Before Elizabeth's time the Inn consisted merely of buildings set around one court, which is now part of Gray's Inn Square. Then wings were added, making two more courts—and by degrees the Inn grew. Between its buildings and Holborn, about 1580, lay an open field and other crofts; and adjoining these on the north a large garden.

There was no attempt at laying out pleasure grounds until after 1586, when Francis Bacon, that great lover of gardens, became a Bencher. His chief interests at the Inn were Masques and Gardens. Of masques he wrote that they "are but toys to come amongst such serious considerations. But yet, since princes will have such things, it is better they should be graced with elegancy than daubed with cost." And the masques he produced were certainly elegant though often also "daubed with cost."

Of the Inns of Court the Inner Temple and Gray's Inn created the finest of these "Revels," and such was the degree of friendship and mutual hospitality between the two Societies that, as a delicate compliment, the winged horse of the Inner Temple was set in carved relief above the gateway of Gray's Inn Square, and, in reciprocation, the griffin placed on the great gate of Inner Temple garden; and there those fabulous beasts may be seen to this day.

Bacon's ideas with regard to gardens were on a large scale. He believed that the perfect garden should comprise not less than 30 acres of ground, and his famous essay, *Of Gardens*, was inspired by Lord Burghley's extensive and greatly-admired garden at Theobald's Park in Hertfordshire. Unlike Sir William Temple and John Evelyn, who also left their mark on horticulture, Bacon had no private garden of his own in which to test his theories and experiments such as are set forth in his *Sylva Sylvarum*, or *Natural Historie in Ten Centuries*. Consequently his writings lack the necessary background of practical experience. This remarkable man, even when Lord Chancellor and busied with great affairs of state, could at any moment bend his intellect to consider methods of growing strawberries, of grafting and watering, of ripening wall fruit. One of his admirers has aptly said, "He could descend from the Woolsack to investigate the economy of manure beds." Gray's Inn gardens were his sole contribution to practical horticulture—but such a contribution that one is conscious of his influence even to-day. Just as the gardens at Hampton Court are still pervaded by the Tudor atmosphere, so the spirit of Francis Bacon seems to haunt Gray's Inn gardens while his statue looks across South Square. They remain pretty much as he made them; and it is interesting to see how many of the features in his Essay he was able to embody here.

Work on the gardens began in 1591, when it was planned "to enclose parts of our back field" with a brick wall; and the arrangements for this were entrusted to Mr. Angel and Mr. Bacon, the latter being then twenty years of age. This "back field" was on the western side of the Inn's property, and eventually became the pleasure garden and "Walks." It was further enlarged in 1608 by the pulling down of certain cottages and stables, but the later erection of Verulam Buildings encroached on it again.

In 1597 an order was issued "that the summe of £7.15.4. due to Mr. Bacon for planting of trees in the walkes be paid next term." As far back as 1583 there had existed no less than 91 elms, a young ash and 3 walnut trees, all properly catalogued, but some of these must have now been past their prime, for in 1598 we find a further order for a "supply of more yonge elme trees in the place of such as are decayed and that a new Rayle and quicksett hedge bee set uppon the upper long walks at the good discretion of Mr. Bacon and Mr. Wilbraham soe that the charges thereof doe not exceed the sum of seventy pounds." And in 1600 there was yet another disbursement of £60 6s. 8d. for the "Garnishing of the walkes"—with ornamental trees, roses and other flowers.

Can you see the enthusiast striving to make his dreams come true? ". . . the garden is best to be square, encompassed on all four sides with a stately arched hedge . . ." As for flowers: "I do hold it in the royal ordering of gardens there ought to be gardens for all the months in the year; in which severally things of beauty may be then in Season . . ." with due regard to the climate of London. His list is too long to reproduce here, but we may be fairly certain that at Gray's Inn he would include daffodils and tulips, "monk's hoods of all colours," columbines, "lilies of all natures," French marigolds, "hollyoaks," and gilliflowers . . . "And because the breath of flowers is far sweeter in the air (where it comes and goes like the warbling of music) than in the hand . . ." there might be "violets blue," whose scent he thought the sweetest of all flowers, musk-roses, sweet-briar, wallflowers, pinks and honeysuckle. Bacon could thus achieve the trees, walks, hedges and flowers of his ideal garden—and surely there were lawns "because nothing is more pleasant to the eye than green grass kept finely shorn."

Although he disliked certain garden features of the day, such as knots, topiary work, vases and statues, he admired mounts, and in 1609 made one in the north-western corner of the garden, and on it erected a summer-house in memory of Jeremy Bentham, a former reader of Gray's Inn. This summer-house was octagonal, with open sides and a roof supported by slender pillars; and from it a view was obtained over open country to the distant wooded heights of Hampstead and High-gate. It remained standing until 1755, when both mount and summer-house were demolished; and at the same time further alterations were made to "the Walkes" (8).

The lovely flight of shallow steps at the northern end is Bacon's work. It led to a terrace which originally had two alcoves, for Charles Lamb refers to them when he bewails "those accursed Verulam Buildings," which, when he first walked in Gray's Inn, "had not encroached upon all the east side of them" (the gardens), "cutting out delicate green crankles, and shouldering away one of two stately alcoves of the terrace. The survivor stands gaping and relationless, as if it remembered its brother."

The beautifully laid-out "Walks" became a fashionable promenade, and continued to be so during the seventeenth and eighteenth centuries. We get glimpses of them through the eyes of other people. Stow described how they "lie open to the air and the enjoyment of a delight-ful prospect of the Fields. And the garden hath been, for many years, much resorted unto by the gentry of both sexes and are the chief orna-ment belonging to the Inn." James Howell, author and diplomat, declared in 1621 that they were "the pleasantest place about London and that you have there the choicest society." Of course Pepys went there, In 1661 he wrote: "Here I to Graye's Inne Walk, all alone, and with great pleasure seeing the fine ladies walk there." And in May, 1662, he was not "all alone": "When church was done, my wife and I walked to Graye's Inne, to observe fashions of the ladies because of my wife making some clothes." But other things took place in the gardens besides fashion parades. A duel was fought in 1701, and the survivor was tried for manslaughter. And later on their privileges were so abused that the gardener was authorized to prevent suspicious persons from entering, and to turn out those who were disorderly.

The gardens are entered by elegant gates of wrought-iron, with griffins surmounting their stone piers. The date of erection, 1723, is plainly visible in the iron-work, and also the arms of the Society and the letters "W.I.G.", which are "the first two letters of his Xtian and surname—William Gilby," the Treasurer at that time. The "T" above his initials stands for "Treasurer" just as "P" stands for "Principal" on some of the gates of other Inns.

Legend has it that the ancient and honourable catalpa tree grew from a seed given to Bacon by Sir Walter Raleigh; but cold historical facts cast doubt on the story, which was not mentioned till 1822, when it appeared in Loudon's Encyclopaedia. Such a new and rare tree could hardly have escaped the notice of gardeners during a period when gardening was fashionable, and novelties sought after and acclaimed. But the catalpa is not mentioned by Gerard in his *Herbal*, nor in the later edition of 1633, edited by Johnson, nor in Parkinson's *Paradisus* in 1629, nor in Evelyn's *Sylva*, 1664—all of them published after Bacon's death. According to the *Botanical Magazine*, the tree was introduced into this country about 1728 by Catesby, a well-known botanist and a member of Sir Hans Sloane's plant-collecting expedition to America. A description of it appeared in his *Natural History of Carolina*, dated 1731. But the celebrated catalpa of Gray's Inn may quite well have been planted within a hundred years of Bacon's death. It has undoubtedly been one of the finest specimens in England, and it still flowers gallantly every year.

During the nineteenth century a great variety of birds frequented the well-wooded grounds—martins, cuckoos, flycatchers, jackdaws, starlings, fieldfares, thrushes, redwings, robins, tits, willow-wrens, hooded crows—and rooks which eventually routed the crows. The rookery in the old elms became famous, and the rooks, as tame as the London pigeons, were fed daily by the inhabitants of the Inn until the end of the century. Now, after a cataclysm that damaged the Inn considerably and banished wild life, the birds are beginning to return to the gardens. A pair of crows nested here in 1946 and 1947, and crows still come to find food. Will these prove to be the founders of another colony? Owls, which probably took refuge in the bombed buildings, fly about the gardens, and are heard hooting at night; and somehow these birds seem to link the Inn with the rural Holborn of long long ago.

The gardens are empty of the fashionable chattering throngs that once eddied along the shady walks and paused to admire and smell the flowers. The venerable elms have gone, and so have the noisy rooks. All is quiet and peaceful. As we take a last lingering look through the tall gates the gardens seem a little withdrawn, as though wrapped in their own memories. Sunlight flickers through the leaves of the plane trees on to the walks and lawns, lighting the shallow steps at the far end; and Charles Lamb's words float into our minds: "They are still the best gardens of any of the Inns of Court, my beloved Temple not forgotten—have the gravest character, their aspect being altogether reverend and law-breathing. Bacon has left the impress of his feet upon their gravel walks."

* * * *

And what of the vanished Inns of Chancery and their gardens?

Once upon a time—that is, in 1756—the garden of Clifford's Inn was a neatly kept and airy spot, "being enclosed with a palisade pale, and adorned with rows of lime trees set round the grass plats and gravel walks." Now it is merely a grassy plot with three or four trees.

The gardens of Furnival's Inn, Thavies', Barnard's and Clement's no longer exist. As for Staple Inn, as long ago as Henry V's reign it was taken for students by Gray's Inn—when it probably looked much the same as it does to-day; and in 1622 was described as having a garden adjoining. To-day, if you pass through an archway set in the lovely timbered and gabled façade of black and white, you will find yourself in a little quiet courtyard of cobblestones and shady trees, flanked on three sides by dignified old red-brick houses with pedimented doorways. And still farther on, beyond the bomb damage, lies another little garden, open and paved, with flower-beds and a fountain and seats.

It is most surprising—yet typical of London, where all sorts of delights are tucked away in hidden places. Bomb damage has exposed the garden's secret on one side, but in Holborn you would never guess that it existed.

CHAPTER III

Conventual Gardens

Charterhouse — Syon House

A SHADY SQUARE of lawns and trees crossed diagonally by paved paths; on the far side an ancient weathered archway, the entrance to the old Carthusian monastery, set in a long stone wall over which mulberry leaves appear; beyond this, glimpses of grey mediaeval buildings with small windows; a tower and a cupola . . .

That is what is seen as one approaches Charterhouse to-day. It is a tantalizing view, suggesting all sorts of possibilities behind that secretive wall. But we may not pass through the gateway because of building operations in progress within, and in a way that leaves the imagination free. We can picture what lies inside the walls without having our vision broken by the harsh realities of concrete and steel scaffolding. Let us sit under the trees in Charterhouse Square and think back to 1349.

That was the year of the Black Death, when people were dying so fast that the churchyards proved insufficient for burials. Accordingly Ralph Stratford, Bishop of London, purchased three acres of land here, where we are sitting, from the Knights Hospitallers, who were near at hand in the Priory of St. John, Clerkenwell. He enclosed it with a brick wall, dedicated it for burials, and built a chapel where masses might be said for the souls of the dead. This spot he called Pardon Churchyard, and for 200 years it was used for the burial of those who died of plague, for executed criminals and suicides. To-day no vestige of it remains, and the very name has passed away.

Almost as soon as this churchyard had been established, Sir Walter Manny bought an adjacent 13-acre plot of ground for the same purpose, and on this, in 1371, the Carthusian monastery was founded by Manny, assisted by Michael Northburgh, Bishop of London. Northburgh was

8   GRAY'S INN: An eighteenth-century bird's-eye view
From an engraving by Sutton Nicholls

9 "THE CHARTER HOUSE"

From an engraving of about 1740 by W. H. Toms

himself a Dominican, but he had seen and known Carthusians abroad, and had a high opinion of the Order. Furthermore, it was peculiarly appropriate that Carthusians should settle here, for their chief duty is prayer for the dead. They are a strictly enclosed and silent Order, with a mode of life rather different from that of most monastic communities: each monk lives in a small detached house or cottage placed in its own little garden. At Charterhouse there were twenty-four of these "cells," two-storied dwellings arranged round the central Great Cloister beside the Prior's house.

Each cell contained a little workroom, a small oratory, a room for sleeping, and a living room; also a storage place for wood. In every cell there was a serving hatch in the wall, through which the monk's food, brought from the kitchen, was passed to him in silence: the brethren only ate in the refectory on Sundays and feast days—still in silence—while chapters from the Bible were read from a pulpit.

The distance from hatch to hatch in Charterhouse was 50 ft., so the little private gardens were a fair size, and were beautifully kept by those monks who delighted in gardening. Prayer was, of course, their chief occupation, but each monk practised a handicraft for recreation: this relieved the strain of isolation. Until the introduction of printing the craft most generally followed was that of transcribing; and we owe many beautiful illuminated manuscripts to the Carthusians.

Besides the little individual gardens there were bigger enclosures. Carthusians are strict vegetarians, and the standard of gardening here at Charterhouse was probably as high as was usual in monastic establishments. The kitchen garden was so fruitful that when the monastery was dissolved in 1538 apples and hay, rose trees, rosemary and bay were mentioned among the lesser spoils—as well as 300 carp. Three loads of bay trees, ninety-one fruit trees, rosemary and other shrubs, as well as a load of hay, went to the King's garden at Chelsea; and Richard Cromwell secured "all such bay trees and grafts" as his gardeners found convenient, a bundle of rose trees, 12 loads of timber, 3 merlin birds "and their appurtenances" (for hawking), besides other items; and the Lord Privy Seal managed to obtain "3 baskets of herbs." So well known and worth while were the evergreens at Charterhouse that two gardeners were sent specially from Hampton Court at the time of the Dissolution to gather "cypers, bayes and yows." It is quite likely that yews and cypresses were found in the churchyards as well as the gardens.

The kitchen garden and orchard lay to the north of the buildings, beyond the Great Cloister and the monastery barns. Here, too, was the wilderness or wild garden where the hay was cut, and where the white-habited monks took their exercise; and a burying ground to receive their bodies. In 1598 Stow wrote: "this burying plot is become a fayre garden retayning the old name." Until a comparatively recent date the eastern part of Clerkenwell, which runs along the north wall of Charterhouse, was still called Wildnerness Row; in 1722 it was known for its hawthorn hedges.

The Dissolution of the monasteries accounted for the disappearance of many beautiful old gardens. Some of them, such as Charterhouse and Syon House, passed into secular hands and were made lovely in a different way; but in many cases the fate of the monasteries was shared by the gardens. Forlorn, weed-grown and trampled under foot, they must have added to the general desolation in London and elsewhere. Many of the Orders were large landowners, and skilled in horticulture as well as in healing. Now both these branches of science were transferred to secular hands: the old days were over.

For nearly three years after the monastery of Charterhouse was dissolved with exceptional brutality it was left deserted. In 1542 it was used as a depository for the King's tents, hunting nets and new pavilion; then it passed through various secular hands. When the Duke of Norfolk owned it, from 1565 to 1611, it was known as Howard House. In 1611 Thomas Sutton bought the property and founded "a hospital for poor brethren and scholars"; and in 1614 the first Foundation Scholars of Charterhouse came into being. Evelyn's impression of the institution is recorded in his diary for April 24th, 1657:

"I also visited the Charterhouse, formerly belonging to the Carthusians, now an old neat fresh solitary college for decayed gentlemen. It has a grove, bowling green, garden, chapel, and a hall where they eat in common."

The monks' wilderness was turned into a cricket ground for part of the school; the kitchen garden, with the orchard that lately had been "the Privie Garden" of the secular mansion, became the Master's garden. Later, the orchard was built over by part of Preacher's Court (9).

In 1872 the school was moved to Godalming, and the Charterhouse premises were taken over by the Merchant Taylors' School: they in their turn sold the property to the Medical School of St. Bartholomew's

Hospital, the present owners. During the last war the old garden was dug up and tons of concrete were poured into it to construct an air-raid shelter for 800 people. This must have saved many lives during the winter of 1940–1. Charterhouse itself was practically destroyed on May 11th, 1941. Now rebuilding is being done on a reduced scale, and a new garden is being planned in the north-west corner of Charterhouse. Only some of the old courts and the weathered walls remain to remind us of the mediaeval garden and the white-robed monks who took their exercise there. The mulberry trees which peep over the wall so alluringly belong to a later date.

*   *   *   *

The story of Syon House begins with a royal repentance. Henry V's past was not altogether blameless, nor was that of his father, and in order to expiate the murder of Richard II, the fifth Henry, on the advice of Chichele, Archbishop of Canterbury, founded the religious houses of Syon, in Middlesex, and Sheen, in Surrey. (The second of these we shall come across later.) The chapter of Syon, granted on Henry's accession in 1415, ran:

"To celebrate divine service for ever, for our estate while we live, and for our soul when we shall have departed this life, and for the souls of our most dear lord and father, Henry, late King of England, and Mary, his late wife, our most dear mother; also for the souls of John, late Duke of Lancaster, our grandfather; and of Blanche, his late wife, and of other of our progenitors, and of all the faithful departed."

This "Monastery of St. Saviour and St. Bridget," as it was called, belonged to the Brigittines, a modified Order of St. Augustine as reformed by St. Brigit of Sweden. It consisted of 60 nuns, 13 priests, 4 deacons and 8 lay brothers. The nuns and monks lived apart, but they shared one chapel with twin choirs connected by a grille, and here prayer and praise and intercession were offered continuously.

Henry V gave to the community his Manor of Isleworth, and Henry VI further enriched them by endowments of land in many parts of the country. In 1431 their original buildings proved too small, and they moved to the beautiful riverside site of the present Syon House. For more than a hundred years this wealthy foundation "abode at the head of all the Convents for women in England in learning, riches and piety"

—so much so that at the Dissolution Henry VIII's commissioners could find little or nothing against the community: the "lady Abbas and susters" (were) "as comfortable in everything as might be devised."

However, in spite of this, the "Daughters of Sion" were expelled in 1539, and retired to a house of their Order in Flanders. Queen Mary recalled them, and gave them back their old home, but at her death they were again exiled. After considerable wandering they finally settled in Lisbon, where they still hold property. The Lisbon community returned to England in 1861, and took up their abode at Syon Abbey, South Brent, Devon.

As for Syon House, after the Dissolution Henry VIII retained the wealthy convent for himself. Here poor unhappy Katherine Howard was imprisoned for three months before her trial and execution; and here Henry's body rested on the way to Windsor where he was buried.

Edward VI gave the estate and the monastery to his uncle, the Lord Protector Somerset, who practically razed the convent buildings to the ground, and erected the present house. This has been little changed externally since his day. though the interior was transformed by Robert Adam during the latter part of the eighteenth century. Of the old convent there remain only an ancient gateway of red brick, and the stone tithe barn, which now has a modern roof. Somerset did not live long to enjoy his new house: after his execution Syon was given to John Dudley, Duke of Northumberland, the father-in-law of Lady Jane Grey. This ill-fated lady and her husband lived here after their marriage, and from Syon she went in semi-state by water to the Tower to be proclaimed Queen.

Had she any premonition of the fate in store for her when she left the house, wrapped in her cloak, and walked with her attendants over the wet grass to the landing stage which was, as now, some distance away? At one end of the grounds, by the riverside, where the Thames bends round from Richmond to Isleworth, stands an elaborate stone boat-house, and inside it lies the skeleton of a barge. It would be easy, but quite untrue, to link these with Lady Jane Grey: both are of a later date.

After the nuns were dispersed, Elizabeth, like her father, kept the rich property in her own hands until she bestowed it on Henry Percy, ninth Earl of Northumberland. Later, the three children of Charles I lived here under the guardianship of the next Earl, and their father, then a prisoner at Hampton Court, was allowed to visit them at Syon.

These are all tragic associations, but Syon has many happier memories —of William Turner, "the Father of English Botany," of John Evelyn, of Queen Anne who, when Princess, stayed here. Evelyn visited Syon in 1665 to attend a Council when Charles II was staying there to escape the Plague which was raging in London. Strangely enough, Evelyn, with his knowledge and love of trees, did not admire the garden. He describes Syon as "built out of an old nunnery of stone, and faire enough but more celebrated for its garden than it deserves; yet there is excellent wall fruite and a pretty fountaine; nothing else extraordinary."

We can forgive Evelyn this disparagement, for very few of the trees which were and are the supreme glory of Syon would have attained any appreciable size at this time, and many were still to be planted. The gardens were one of the first examples in England of "a collection of trees and shrubs cultivated as objects of beauty and taste."

The grounds were laid out by the Lord Protector Somerset, who was keenly interested in botany, and it is quite likely that the work was done under the superintendence of Dr. William Turner, whom Somerset made his chaplain and physician. Turner dated his *Names of Herbes* (1548) from Syon, and made frequent references therein to its gardens. There were originally larged walled enclosures on the east and west sides of the house, and, in the angle where they met, a high mount commanding a lovely view of the river. When Somerset was attainted for treason this mount was declared to be a fortification, and was destroyed. A beautiful cedar now stands on the spot.

These old formal gardens were completely swept away when "Capability" Brown re-designed the grounds, and to-day Syon, stately in its four-square simplicity, looks across the river from a dignified setting of trees and lawns: its lake is invisible (10). The changing play of light on flat façades and square corner towers turns the house from golden-grey to cream and then to pearl-grey against its green background. From Kew, across the river, it appears as a beautiful wraith-like vision.

Between the lawns and the river-bank lies what is known as the tide-field, which absorbs the flood-water of the Thames, and a tide-wall that further restrains the overflow, so that the house, though low-lying, is secure against flooding. But the lake is affected by the river; and high tide in the Thames means high water in the lake, and soggy paths alongside.

For the lover of trees Syon is a paradise: it is a thrilling experience to wander about the grounds and discover tree after tree valuable for its rarity or age. The height and spread of the trees is remarkable. They are not elbowed by their neighbours, but have plenty of space in which to attain their true proportions; and being so near the river they can obtain the maximum nourishment for their roots. The result is sometimes breath-taking.

Oldest of all, and oldest in England are the famous mulberry bushes which were brought from Persia in 1548—that would be during the tenancy of the Protector. We are accustomed to see mulberry *trees*, but here are dome-shaped *bushes* higher than a man and of great circumference. Inevitably they suggest, "Here we go round the mulberry bush!" And they are still heavily laden with fruit every year.

It is impossible to say exactly when some of Syon's trees were planted. The catalogue only gives the date of introduction into this country. But we may be sure that as the gardens held one of the earliest collections of trees, specimens would be obtained as speedily as possible. One of the holm oaks (*Quercus ilex*) was probably planted in the sixteenth century. There are at least twenty-eight varieties of oak in the grounds— with an equal variety in the shape and serration of their leaves. Some of the tulip trees (*Liriodendron tulipfera*) date from 1650, and the cedars of Lebanon from 1670. From a distance the latter trees often appear to be bearing astonishing fruits, but closer investigation shows these to be merely herons roosting on the flat tops of the cedars: there is a large heronry there.

Syon possesses the biggest sweet gum (*Liquidambar styraciflua*) known in cultivation. It is well over 90 feet in height, and dates from about 1681. Another tree of which Syon has the finest specimens is the deciduous or swamp cypress (*Taxodium distichum*). The biggest of these, planted about 1640, is more than 111 feet high, and most beautiful with its feathery, bright green foliage. The peculiarity of the swamp cypress is its "knees'—extremely hard woody growths like stalagmites —which are sent up singly or in groups from the widespread roots. The function of these "knees" is a matter for conjecture: one explanation is that, as the tree grows in the swampy regions of the southern U.S.A., they may help to anchor it more firmly to the ground;

another suggestion is that the tree breathes by means of these woody projections.

Near the lake are two very large Zelkovas (*Zelkova crenata*) which go back to some time about 1760. These are Caucasian beeches that change to rich colours in autumn. They are extremely hard in texture, and if the trunk is tapped it gives forth a metallic ring. Also beside the lake is a huge and beautiful tree, *Pterocarya caucasia*, rather like a large-leaved ailanthus, but hung with impressive out-sized green catkins about a foot long.

How humble these magnificent old trees make us feel! Man's life is but a short span of three-score years and ten: the life of a tree is reckoned in hundreds of years—and even then its usefulness is not always ended, for it may enter upon a new phase as timber.

One could go on endlessly enumerating glorious trees at Syon (the catalogue lists 263 trees and shrubs exclusive of varieties), but a few must suffice for now. The best plan is to go and see them for oneself. The house and gardens are thrown open during the summer months by kind permission of his Grace the Duke of Northumberland.

Now for our last tantalizing few trees. We should not miss the huge Constantinople hazel (*Corylus colurna*), introduced in 1665, the sophoras (*Sophora japonica*), and the Judas tree (*Cercis siliquastrum*) on which the traitor disciple is supposed to have hanged himself. A Judas tree in springtime is a marvellous sight, for the bare branches and twigs are smothered in purplish-pink blossoms like small everlasting-peas. There is a fine "cucumber tree" (*Magnolia acuminata*), there are false acacias (*Robina pseudacacia*), a very old cork oak (*Quercus suber*) that was introduced about 1699, maidenhair trees (*Gingko biloba*), black walnuts, cut-leaved alders, pines and maples of many kinds. . . .

At one time every tree bore a leaden tag with its name and species clearly set out, but these labels began to disappear mysteriously, nobody could think how or why: it was most baffling. And then fragments of inscribed lead with tiny teeth marks were found in the grass: the squirrels (whose digestions must be abnormal!) had nibbled away the tags right to the suspending wires—when, of course, the labels dropped off. That explains the shortage of descriptive tags on the trees to-day.

Syon had its war casualties in the grounds. Bombs fell and destroyed some trees: others, especially beeches, were scarred by shrapnel, and in certain specimens the shrapnel is still embedded.

At one side of the house is a prettily laid-out flower garden with an elegant crescent-shaped conservatory by Sir William Paxton, the designer of the Crystal Palace. On the terrace outside are arranged florid stone vases said to be the work of Grinling Gibbons. A lilied pool with a fountain jet rising round a lightly poised Mercury, and huge magnolias (*Magnolia conspicua*) add to the charm of this secluded spot. But it is the older part of the grounds and the great trees that most truly breathe the spirit of Syon.

CHAPTER IV

Ecclesiastical Gardens

Lambeth Palace — Fulham Palace

To what degree have gardens influenced the course of history? It is impossible to say; but flowers and bird-song, trees and green lawns do undoubtedly have an effect upon our mental and emotional processes. A certain busy London doctor used to slip away from town whenever possible to spend the night with a friend in the country who had a beautiful garden; and at six o'clock the next morning the gardeners would find the doctor walking among the flowers, absorbing their dewy scented freshness and the sparkling wetness of lawns, listening to the passionate bird-chorus that came from trees still half-wrapped in misty veils. He would explain to the surprised gardeners that he was visiting the flowers "for the necessary refreshment of mind and body": and would go back to London ready for another heavy day's work.

That being the case with one private individual, what must be the cumulative effect of gardens on kings and queens, prelates and statesmen? For all we know, harsh judgments may have been softened, justice been tempered with mercy, revenge abandoned. At any rate, it is good to think so. And that brings us to two ecclesiastical gardens, and some of the great personages who walked therein and had to make important decisions. The gardens of Lambeth Palace and Fulham Palace are full of human interest.

At Lambeth the garden to-day, lying in the shadow of the old Palace with its battlemented towers, gives no hint of rich historical associations save for one feature that we shall come to presently. The terrace certainly belongs to the past—it was there in Laud's time—but its present charming arrangement of grass and flagstones broken by flower-beds dates only from the days of Archbishop Lang. There is a small modern rose garden, and more beds are filled with flowers: for the rest, the garden of ten acres or so has a park-like aspect, and provides an admirable stage setting for ecclesiastical drama. The trees—ailanthus, catalpa, copper beech, sycamore and planes—are fairly young; only a couple of hollow-trunked elms, both at least 200 years old, tell of former plantings. Everything else has disappeared.

But the Palace garden in the fourteenth century was a different place. It included the adjacent nine acres now leased to the London County Council for the nominal rent of 1s. a year, and known as Archbishop's Park. Several small streams ran into the Thames here, and a moat enclosed the property, which extended to the river where the Archbishop had his barge-house. There was the usual "Great Garden" surrounded by a wall thatched with reeds, a flower garden, a rabbit garden with a protecting hedge round it, and a cygnet-house for the swans which, with the rabbits, helped to vary the diet. Vines were grown; and herbs in the garden included "olearum, fletrocilii, shervil, clarey, littuse, spynhach, toncressin, cabache, concumber and gourds, isope, bourage, centurrage." How odd our familiar vegetables appear when masquerading in this old spelling!

When we come to the sixteenth century the gardens are peopled with famous figures—Sir Thomas More, Latimer, Cranmer, Cardinal Pole among them. During More's trial at Lambeth Palace he was at one point ordered to leave the judgment hall and go down into the garden. The April days were unduly warm, and More tells us, "I tarried in the old burned chamber that looketh downe to the garden and would not goe down because of the heat in that time." While he "tarried" he saw Latimer walking in the garden with other doctors and chaplains, "and very merry I saw him, for he laughed and took one or twain about the neck so handsomely that if they had been women I would have weened that he had waxed wanton."

Latimer lodged at the Palace for some time, and a letter from him to Edward VI shows that even in the sixteenth century people suffered tiresome interruptions.

"I walk in the Garden looking at my book, as I can do but little good at it. But something I must needs do to satisfy the place. I am no sooner in the Garden and have read awhile but by-and-by cometh there someone knocking at the gate. Anon cometh my man and saith, 'Sir, there is one at the gate would speak with you.'"

If a certain letter to Queen Elizabeth can be believed, the Palace garden was the scene of a most poignant incident. The writer was one

Dr. Aless, a Leipzig professor living in London, and he dreamed vividly on the eve of Anne Boleyn's execution that he saw her headless body. Terrified, he rose at once and went to Lambeth, where he found Cranmer already up and walking restlessly in the garden. (Mrs. Dorothy Gardiner gives the story in Aless's own words.)

"When the Archbishop saw me he inquired why I had come so early, for the clock had not yet struck four. I told him the whole occurrence. He continued in silent wonder for awhile and at length broke out into these words, 'Do you not know what is to happen to-day?' And when I answered that I had remained at home since the date of the Queen's imprisonment, and knew nothing of what was going on, the Archbishop then raised his eyes to heaven and said, 'She who has been Queen of England upon earth will to-day become a Queen in heaven.' So great was his grief that he could say nothing more, and then burst into tears. . . ."

Whether the story is true or not, one feels that Cranmer must have suffered great distress of mind, for, he said, I "had loved her not a little for the love I judged her to bear towards God and his gospel."

In Cranmer's time there was a beautiful summer-house in the garden, designed by his chaplain, Dr. John Ponet or Poynet. After being repaired by Archbishop Parker this building gradually fell into decay and was removed. Now nobody even knows where it stood. Cranmer's hospitality was lavish, and it is pleasant to have a glimpse of him at home. One visitor wrote, "We often sing here at the Archbishop's, who is extremely fond of music." With so much entertaining Lambeth had to be self-supporting on a large scale. Grain was harvested and stored until it was taken to the miller: it seems rather curious to find bread being baked for the horses as well as for the household. Cattle and sheep evidently abounded, for they supplied "Bifes, Muttons and Veales; their hides were marketed. Crabs" (crab-apples) "to be crushed for verjuice, broken voynes" (grapes) "for vinegar": there were fruits, cheese and junkets, "Gellies, Pottage and other subtilities" with a drop of wine for flavouring.

Archbishop (later Cardinal) Pole provided a link which spans the centuries and joins the sixteenth to the twentieth. Some time during his Primacy (1554–8) he planted the famous fig trees. These were injured during a hard winter in the early part of the nineteenth century, and had to be cut down nearly to the ground; but they have since flourished exceedingly, and to-day form a thick, shrubby screen outside the south wall of the old library. In fact, the trees are emulating the banyan in that many of the branches are layering themselves. To step behind that barrier of fig leaves is to find oneself in a green, twilit jungle of twisting branches and dense foliage. There are about five trees, and all but one are the white Marseilles variety that ripen deliciously and in profusion, and can be preserved as well as eaten raw. The exception is a black Turkey fig that does not attain perfection in this country: it is apt to be hard and "pippy."

An able wife is as great a help to an Archbishop as to any other man, and Mistress Parker was affectionately known as "Parker's Abbess." The rules drawn up for their Graces' gardener show very clearly the methodical mind of a good housewife:

"His office is to see the garden, orchard and walks to be kept well weeden, rould, the grass walks and platts not suffered to be much growne but kept lowe with the sythe. To see that there be planted in the grounds flowers, hearbs and roots, both for the provision of the kitchen and chambers; and with all sorts of good fruits, hearbs, plants and flowers for use and pleasure. That he keep nurseries of all sorts of good plants, to supply any defect that may happen, and that he delve and manure the grounds to the best commodity of the owner."

The fig trees were not the only long-lived inhabitants of the garden. Archbishop Laud placed a tortoise there, and it survived till 1751, finally perishing, through the carelessness of a gardener, at the mature age of 110 years.

Laud had a special fondness for Lambeth, and loved the river in all its moods. His diary reflects the changing conditions of high tides, low water, the freezing of the river, and a "most extream tempest on the Thames." After his death in 1647 a valuation of his property was made, and this gives us a good idea of the garden at the time. Pole's gallery is mentioned "with a tarras walke under it open towards the garden." The flower garden was "foure square, and Walled about on the north and west sides with Brickwalls." On its eastern side lay an orchard "sett with Apple Trees, Paire Trees, Plum Trees, and moated round about." Along the north wall ran the "longe tarras walke paved with square Tyles, opening with arches" into the garden, and over this terrace an upper leaden promenade and a "Bankuetting house" (a favourite garden feature of the period). There were also two fish-ponds and a great number of elms, walnut and chestnut trees.

10 SYON HOUSE from Kew Gardens in 1832

Engraved after J. Farington, R.A., for "An History of the River Thames," II

11   LAMBETH PALACE: Seen from across the Thames about 1720
From an engraving by J. Kip, after L. Knyff

After Laud's death there was no Archbishop living at Lambeth until the Restoration, for the See of Canterbury was vacant. And then the aspect of the garden seems to have changed considerably with succeeding changes of ownership (11). Sancroft was not interested in the grounds, and neglected them, but his successor, Tillotson (1691–5), was a keen gardener and believed in keeping up with the times. He ordered the very latest and most fashionable gardening fancy, to wit, " a green-house, one of the finest and costliest about the town. It is of 3 rooms, the middle having a stove under it." This greenhouse was, however, badly situated so that it got very little sunshine in winter. All the same, it seems to have fulfilled its purpose adequately, for the description goes on to say, "Most of the greens are oranges and lemons, which have very large ripe fruit on them."

Here we see the Dutch influence at work. William III was a keen gardener, and introduced gardening features from his native land—neat, precise flower-beds, little standard trees in tubs, as we have seen in the Temple gardens, clipped or pleached arbours, topiary work, and of course tulips. All these gave a stiff and formal air to gardens, and were immensely popular with the English.

Right up to 1750 there was a moat round the outer part of the Lambeth property, and more water, another moat or "serpentine canal," round the inner garden. When Thomas Secker arrived on the scene in 1758 these stretches of water were scummy and green with weed, and flowers and fruit were sadly lacking elsewhere. But the new Archbishop soon put things right. Let us glance at the garden in his time. Lambeth is still practically in the country, with pleasant lanes round about, and an inmate of the Palace household is writing to a friend in the 1760's:

"Going to Fulham" (which was even more rural) "has made this place quite a town. It is a town of blooms and perfumes, however. The forecourt, inhabited by full 200 very amusing chickens, is quite fragrant with lime-blossoms . . . jessamine . . . cluster round the windows: the rose-walk is to-day in its highest bloom. At every spot one moves to in the garden is some variety of sweets; here a gale of spicy pinks; there the breath of lillies . . ."

And on another occasion: the "whole border of the serpentine canal is filled with single pinks, red and white, which perfume the air and look sweet and soft beyond imagination."

There could not be a more enchanting picture with which to take our leave of Lambeth Palace garden: anything further would be an anti-climax.

*   *   *   *

The name "Fulham" signifies "home of birds": in its original form, "Volucrum Domus," the literal translation was "habitacle of birds." This is easily credible, for in far-off times, when the Danes one winter dug the moat (of the present Bishop's house) to keep off the Saxons, Fulham was wild marsh-land, and consequently a great haunt of birds. As late as 1521 it was reported that herons and spoonbills were building their nests in the Palace grounds—but grounds that were very different in appearance from to-day's garden. In 1439–40 there was mention of the "house husbondrie" or home farm, the great garden, the "vyne garden" and a wood; also a hayloft, stable and larder. The estate must have resembled a prosperous farm.

There have been Bishops of London living at Fulham since pre-Conquest days, and their occupation has been continuous except for fifteen years during the Commonwealth. For a considerable period Fulham was their country residence, and they had another house in town. Originally the Palace estate comprised forty or fifty acres of land surrounded by the moat that the Danes dug. The site of this moat was given to Fulham Borough Council by Bishop Winnington-Ingram in 1924, and has been laid out as an ornamental garden. Eighty years ago a strip of land between the moat and the river was given away, and is now a public garden known as Bishop's Park. These concessions have reduced the grounds of the Palace to eighteen acres; but the spirit of a bygone age still haunts the garden.

It greets one at the very threshold, where a low, arched gateway leads to the quiet courtyard surrounded by Tudor buildings of red brick lozenged with black burnt bricks of that time, and where small windows look down on to a fountain in the centre. This peaceful quadrangle was rebuilt by Bishop Fitzjames in 1521. Thence, by way of the porch, with a clock and Bishop Juxon's arms over it, and through the old part of the Palace, where painted portraits of royalties and ecclesiastical dignitaries look down benignly from the walls, we come to the garden with its wide velvety lawns, old trees, winding paths and other delights.

Peace broods over the garden—a peace that is only emphasized by rapturous bird-song—and in the stillness and fragrance and hot sun-shine the past lays hold of us; we are transported to other centuries, and can imagine the former bishops strolling across the lawn in ruffs or white bands, and enjoying the garden in their several ways.

Bishop Bonner, that fanatical persecutor of heretics in Mary's reign, seems to have used the grounds for a somewhat unusual purpose. He spent much time therein "not from the love of its repose," but because he could remain undisturbed while "with rod or by equally stringent measures" he strove to "persuade" followers of the reformed religion to recant. A favourite resort was at the end of a winding path in a shrubbery, known as Monk's Walk, and there he used to sit in a chair to examine heretics. On one occasion he sent for two willow wands, and made a stubborn youth "to kneel against a long bench in an arbour." Then he beat him "till for weariness he was obliged to leave off." Another young man was similarly treated, the Bishop "having him to his orchard, there, within a little arbour, with his own hands beat him with a willow wand."

What anguish—of body as well as soul—the garden must have wit-nessed! Bonner's reputation for cruelty was so great that Elizabeth refused to let him kiss her hand at her accession. He must have had some strong feeling for Fulham, for it is reported that his burly ghost haunts the Palace to this day.

It was for quite other and happier reasons that Bishop Grindal, Bonner's successor, frequented the garden. He was a great horticulturist, like Bacon and Burghley at this time. It was Grindal who introduced the tamarisk into this country. He planted a slip at Fulham, and although it died long ago there are now cuttings of tamarisk growing in the adjacent public gardens—a pleasant tribute to the Bishop's memory. Grindal used to send Queen Elizabeth presents of choice fruit from the garden; and on one awful occasion was suspected of sending some when one of the Palace servants had the plague. However, this was proved to be a false alarm. In 1566 Grindal wrote to Lord Burghley apologizing that he had "no fruit to offer him but some grapes." No apology can have been needed, for at that time the vines at Fulham were famous, and the grapes there ripened earlier and more deliciously than anywhere else.

The next Bishop, Aylmer, cared nothing for the garden; in fact, Aubrey says that "he cutt down a noble crowd of trees at Fulham," amongst them being many fine elms. This drew down upon him the Queen's displeasure (which troubled him exceedingly), and she forbade any further depredations. Aylmer was fond of bowls, and used to play on Sunday afternoons after evening prayer. His language when he grew excited over the game was said to be such "as exposed him to the censure of many, especially of his enemies"—though the present generation would not be shocked at such an expletive as "The devil go with it!" However, it was considered wise to keep visitors away from the worthy divine while he was playing bowls.

When the Palace was sold by the Parliament in 1647 to Col. Edmund Harvey, the deed of sale described it as the site of the manor with

"one private chappell, and all buildings, outhouses, dove-houses, barnes, stables, granaries, coach-houses, courts, courtyards, orchards, gardens, walkes, fish-ponds, pumps, water-courses thereto belonging, and 2 footbridges, and 1 great bridge" (across the Thames) "and 3 closes of pasture called the warren, which premises are all encompassed with a moat . . . and doe conteyne together within the saide moate thirtie-six acres and a half by admeasurement."

This extensive property contained about 700 trees, as well as osier beds and the right of salmon fishing.

The Bishop who did most for the gardens (not excepting Grindal) was Compton. His episcopate lasted from 1675 to 1714, and thus he was able to see the result of much of his work. Moreover, though he was appointed to the See of London in Charles II's reign, as an ardent Protestant he was suspended when James II came to the throne, and could not resume his duties until the accession of William and Mary. Those years of retirement he spent at Fulham, and made the already famous garden his chief interest. What he accomplished there interested his contemporaries. Evelyn wrote in his Diary on October 11th, 1681: "To Fulham to visit the Bishop of London, in whose garden I first saw the *Sedum arborescens* in flower which was exceedingly beautiful." (This plant is now known as *Cotyledon orbiculata*: an old-fashioned and erroneous name for it was Round-leaved Navelwort.)

Another visitor, Switzer (who worked in the royal gardens at Hampton Court), noted in his *Iconographia Rustica* in 1718:

"He" (Compton) "had a thousand species of exotick plants in his stoves and gardens, in which last place he had endizoned a great many that have been formerly thought too tender for this cold climate." (One of these was the passion-flower.) "There were few days in the year, till towards the latter part of his life, but he was actually in his garden, ordering and directing the Removal and Replacing of his Trees and plants."

Not only that: the good Bishop spread abroad the knowledge that he had acquired, and freely admitted students of botany and horticulture to the grounds of Fulham. The most eminent gardeners and botanists visited him there.

Compton was also tutor to the Princess Mary (afterwards Queen) and Princess Anne. He played an important part in bringing William of Orange to England, and when Sancroft, Archbishop of Canterbury, refused to officiate at the coronation, performed the ceremony himself. To Compton Mary probably owed her love of gardening, and she and William no doubt consulted him about the gardens at Hampton Court and Kensington.

Fulham has always been noted for its fine trees, and it was Bishop Compton who introduced many of them. A paper read before the Royal Society in 1757 listed 37 varieties, including the black Virginian walnut tree, flowering ash, cluster pine, red horse-chestnut, honey locust, cotton tree, evergreen oak, false acacia, Virginian sumach, cut-leaved jessamine, Virginian flowering maple. There may have been an olive tree and a pistachio; there certainly was a cork tree (now dead), and a stately avenue of elms which led to the Palace (but no longer exists). At the end of this avenue were "the Bishop's Steps" where the episcopal barge was moored when not in use.

Alas, Compton was followed by Robinson, who largely undid his predecessor's work. He removed all the greenhouse plants, the delicate exotics and many of the rarer shrubs and trees to make room for the ordinary vegetables and fruit of the kitchen garden. But Bishop Porteus (1787–1809) planted cedars, and Bishop Blomfield an ailanthus (Tree of Heaven) and a deciduous cypress.

Although the honey locust and practically all the older trees have died, Fulham can still show beautiful specimens. An immense and aged plane is said by some to be the first planted in England—but it has several rivals. In any case, it is probably about 300 years old. There are two great cedars, mulberry trees and a catalpa, and what might be the surviving remains of the false acacia. A Turkey oak and a fern-leaf beech are fine examples of their kind, as is also a huge old spreading ilex or evergreen oak. This may well be the original tree, for its main trunk is a ruin, and several more trunks have grown up close around it from the same roots.

Beyond the great lawn with its lovely trees an old wall of warm red Tudor bricks encloses a vast kitchen garden with a gay herbaceous-bordered walk down the centre. This, one feels, has remained unchanged since the days of Bishop Fitzjames, who built the wall. Now, as in his time, fruit trees are snowy with bloom in springtime; now, as then, bees and butterflies disport themselves on hot summer days when the scent of flowers hangs drowsily in the air. An archway in this wall, surmounted by the Fitzjames crest in stone, and heavily overhung with wistaria, leads to a knot garden, its box-edged beds filled with roses. And the wistaria, a garlanded hedge, continues as a boundary all along one side of the knots.

Outside the wall lie beds of irises and other flowers, little rambling gardens, the orchard (near which was the Monk's Walk), and a wood of mixed trees. A path runs right round the wall and leads us through the wood and back to the garden and its brooding quiet. Of Fulham Bishop Blomfield truly said that it is "a house dearly loved, so close upon the restless world, yet itself a haunt of ancient peace."

CHAPTER V

Citizens' Gardens

A ND what, we may ask, was happening to the humbler folk of London while the religious orders, the prelates and noblemen were cultivating and enjoying their great estates? What of the "common man" and his patch of ground? Londoners were ever garden-lovers, and we have seen how at the turn of the twelfth and thirteenth centuries even the "Town Ditche" was stopped up with houses and gardens built thereon.

In early times there was no town-planning: the small dwellings of the City were built to please their individual owners, and consequently were set at all angles, facing different directions. The winding ways between were only footpaths or alleys, and wherever spaces occurred among the houses they were cultivated. FitzStephen, the historian who lived in Henry II's reign, gives us a glimpse of London in the twelfth century: "Everywhere without the Houses of the Suburbs, the Citizens have Gardens and Orchards planted with trees, large, beautiful, and one joining to another."

As most of the land in the City was occupied by convent properties, the only open space the people could get for sport and recreation was "the great fen or moor on the north of the city wall." This "Moor-fields" was a place of resort for 800 years. At first merely a marshy ground largely covered with ponds and rushes (like Smithfield or "Smooth-field" at the same period), it was "much used for exercise in shooting of bows and arrows and all sorts of sport." The erection of the "Moor-gate" in 1415 gave easier access for the people; and in 1527 the marsh was drained, and became increasingly popular. In 1606 the Fields were laid out rather like a public garden, and continued to be one of the chief places of recreation for the citizens until the end of the eighteenth century. Displays and sham fights were held there, and Pepys describes a contest at Moorfields in 1664 between the butchers and weavers, in which the weavers were victorious. During the Great Fire crowds of homeless people camped there in great anxiety.

FitzStephen gives us a description of winter sports that has the lovely detail of a Breughel painting:

"When that great Moor which washeth Moorfields . . . is frozen over, great Companies of Young Men go to sport upon the Ice: then fetching a Run, and setting their feet at a distance, and placing their Bodies sideways they slide a great Way. Others take heaps of Ice, as if it were great Millstones and make Seats: Many going before draw him that sits thereon, holding one another by the Hand: in going so fast, some slipping with their feet all fall down together, some are better practised to the Ice and bind to their shoes Bones as the legs of some Beasts, and hold Stakes in their hands headed with sharp Iron, which sometimes they strike against the Ice."

(It was not until the reign of Charles II that modern skates came into fashion: before that time polished bones were used.)

By the end of the fourteenth century the City had become a congested place of narrow streets and gabled houses two or three stories high, with their frontages set at different depths from the street. From the streets ran even narrower courts, so it is not surprising that under these over-crowded and insanitary conditions epidemics broke out. Rich and poor huddled side by side, and every house of importance had its garden.

None of the mediaeval gardens survives to-day; but in old pictures, tapestries and illuminations we can see what they were like. There was generally a square enclosure with walls of clay, brick or stone, or a thick hedge round it. A favourite device was a raised bank of earth against the wall, faced with brick or stone, and planted on top with sweet-smelling herbs. This bank was often broken by recesses containing turfed seats. The garden was laid out in rectangular beds where herbs and flowers grew together, trees, and plots of thyme or camomile for lawns: grass lawns were rare until Elizabeth's reign, thyme and camomile being preferred because when trodden upon they gave out their scent. Gravelled paths intersected the garden, and it usually contained an arbour and a cistern or fountain.

The flowers grown would be rather limited in variety, and would include, besides those mentioned in monastic gardens, periwinkle, violet, monkshood and Chaucer's daisy. But there would be an abundance of herbs for seasoning meat—onions, leeks, garlic, fennel, mint, parsley, saffron, cabbages; and fruit included cherries, strawberries, apples, pears, medlars (which, as now, were kept till "bletted" or rotten before being eaten), and also inferior peaches and quinces.

The gardens, large and small, were so productive that a market for the sale of surplus "pulse, cherries, vegetables, and other wares to their trade pertaining" used to be held opposite the church of St. Austin (St. Augustine) near the gate of St. Paul's churchyard. But by 1345 this market had become very large and crowded, so that it hindered passing pedestrians and horsemen; and the "scurrility, clamour and nuisance of the gardeners and their servants" became so objectionable to the residents in those parts, and such "a nuisance to the priests who are singing Matins and Mass in the church of St. Austin, and to others, both clerks and laymen, in prayers and orisons there serving God," that the Mayor and Aldermen were petitioned to interfere and have the market removed to a more suitable spot.

An order was accordingly given to that effect. But the "gardeners of the Earls, Barons and Bishops, and of the citizens of the same city" were not so easily defeated. They in their turn petitioned the Mayor to reverse his order, and eventually were allowed to sell their wares in "the space between the south gate of the churchyard of St. Austin's, and the garden wall of the Friars Preachers at Baynard Castle . . . and nowhere else."

No doubt business went briskly here, but the traders must have missed the traffic and possible customers that streamed into the City through Ludgate and past their former marketing place.

Gardens, of whatever size, were a great refuge for the women of that period: they had perforce to spend most of their time at home, and the garden provided a welcome change from the small, ill-ventilated rooms of the house. The wives and daughters of the London merchants tended their herbs and plucked their fruit; they sang and danced in the garden, played with their pets, did their needlework and entertained their friends there.

Along the riverside there was more elbow-room than in the heart of the City; and here stood the palaces of bishops, abbots and great lords— Essex House, the Temple, Arundel House and so on—each with its gardens, terraces and spacious courts, each with its water-gate and flight of steps down into the river. Westward from Ludgate the ground sloped to the Fleet River and its bridge, a few large houses, shops and taverns; then came the Strand and its "glittering streams." The city wall had been much patched and repaired, and near Aldersgate stood a picturesque group of buildings—the Hospital and Priory of St. Bartholomew, the houses of the Knights Hospitallers and the nuns of Clerkenwell—half-hidden among trees and gardens.

For many centuries the citizens of London continued to enjoy their private gardens (12). The city was expanding, and Stow describes the new suburbs just outside Bishopsgate in the sixteenth century:

"Hogge Lane . . . within these fortie yeares had on both sides fayre hedgerows of Elme trees, with bridges and easie stiles to pass over into the pleasant fields, very commodious for Citizens therein to walke, shoote and otherwise to recreate and refresh their dulled spirites in the sweete and wholesome ayre, which is now within few yeares made a continuall building throughout, of Garden houses, and small Cottages: the fields on either side be turned into Garden plottes, teynter yards, Bowling Allyes, and such like, from Houndes Ditch in the West, so farre as white Chappell, and further towards the East."

Just as the Tudor period was the golden age for music and literature, so it proved to be the golden age of horticulture. The Wars of the Roses were over, and England was at peace; that meant that people had leisure to be interested in their gardens. The discovery of the New World stimulated trade and enterprise—travellers brought home plants from foreign countries: tobacco, the potato, crown imperial, fritillary, lilac or "pipe-tree," spiderwort, sunflower, larkspur and a host of other flowers arrived. Religious persecution drove the Huguenots, notably weavers and gardeners, into this country from Spain, France and the Low Countries. They brought with them new plants and new ideas about gardening; they started flower societies and set up market gardens at Battersea, Bermondsey and elsewhere. The invention of printing made possible more books, including those on herbs and horticulture. People's minds were awakening to a fuller knowledge of the world they lived in, and to a desire for learning. The Reformation took place—and that had a considerable effect on gardening.

Great landowners were not the only people to be keen; the enthusiasm spread to lesser folk, and we find Stow complaining of the "inclosure of the fields in 1516

"for Gardens wherein are builded many fayre summer houses, and as in other places of the Suburbs, some of them like Midsomer Pageantes, with Towers,

Turrets, and Chimney tops, not so much for use or profite, as for shewe and pleasure, bewraying the vanity of men's mindes, much unlike to the disposition of the ancient Cittizens, who delighted in the building of Hospitals and Almes houses for the poore, and therein both imployed their wits and spent their wealthes in preferment of the common commodities of this our Citie."

The mediaeval garden gradually became the pleasure garden of the Tudor age, and was designed as a setting for the house. Formality was still the key-note, and, as Stowe notes, many fascinating conceits were introduced (13). We cannot fully appreciate individual gardens unless we know something of the contemporary fashions, which were extraordinarily interesting. One of the earliest was the railed flower-bed, enclosed by low railings or trellis-work: we shall meet this style presently at Hampton Court, that supreme remaining example of Tudor gardening.

Topiary work was another novelty. This art was known to the Romans, though we do not hear of it being used in England until the time of the Tudors; it made up for its late arrival by remaining fashionable for two centuries. Opinions have differed about this artificial treatment of trees and shrubs. Bacon wrote, "I for my part, do not like images cut in juniper or other garden stuff—they be for children. Little low hedges round like welts, with some pretty pyramids I like well, and in some places fair columns." Bacon also disapproved of knots, one of the most charming fancies of Tudor times: ". . . they be but toys; you may see as good sights many times in tarts." But perhaps he was only thinking of box-edged beds filled with sand or "divers coloured earths" instead of flowers. These narrow beds planned in geometrical patterns and edged with lavender, thrift, rosemary or box, must have looked lovely when crammed with flowers, and smelt delicious when full of herbs: the Elizabethans mixed their flowers like posies.

There seems to have been no limit to the ingenuity of gardeners at this time: they made artificial mounts, arbours or "roosting places" (sometimes high up in trees:), pleached alleys and mazes; "galleries," which were passages roofed with climbing plants; and alleys planted underfoot with fragrant herbs. In his Essay, *Of Gardens*, Bacon suggests that "those which perfume the air most delightfully, not passed by as the rest, but being trodden upon and being crushed are three; that is, burnet, wild thyme, and water-mints. . . ." Sundials, fountains and ponds, though not new, continued to be popular, as did the turfed seats on banks.

Many of these features would be found in the smaller London gardens of the period. Now let us see what the gardens and orchards produced. New flowers in Elizabeth's reign included asphodel, bachelors' buttons, pansies or heartsease, marigolds, lilies of the valley, snapdragon, jasmine, sweet-william, French broom, rosemary, hollyhocks, lilac, laburnum, nasturtium, tulips, love-in-a-mist, martagon lilies, sunflowers.

The flower gardens of England in the sixteenth century have been immortalized and made fragrant for ever by Shakespeare and Spenser. And in their day one did not have to travel far afield for flowers: London was small, and though congested still, had its gardens where flowers grew unpolluted by smoke and factory chemicals in the air. Even Holborn, where Gerard had his garden, was still rural; and Shakespeare might have been describing an enclosed London garden with its planted banks and pretty arbour when he wrote:

> "I know a bank whereon the wild thyme blows,
>   Where ox-lips and the nodding violet grows;
>   Quite over-canopied with lush woodbine,
>   With sweet musk-roses and with eglantine."

In such a garden he would find "hot lavender, mints, savory, marjoram,"—"rosemary . . . for remembrance,"—"pale primroses, that die unmarried,"—"streak'd gillyvors,"—"dangling apricocks,"—"honeysuckles ripened by the sun." And for his wild flowers he would not need to go back to his native Warwickshire: the lanes around Gray's Inn, the open country on the north towards Highgate, and on the west towards Chelsea, would yield "lady smocks all silver white, and cuckoo buds of yellow hue" (marsh marigolds), "the azured harebell," "crowflowers, nettles, daisies and long purples" (which were probably wild orchis).

How quaint and lovely some of the old flower names were can be seen in Spenser's *Ditty in praise of Eliza, Queen of the Shepherds.*

> "Bring hether the Pincke and purple Cullambine,
>   With Gilliflowers;
>   Bring Coronations, and Sops-in-wine
>   Worn of Paramoures:

Strow me the ground with Daffadowndillies,
And Cowslips, and Kingcups, and lovèd Lillies:
The pretie Pawnce,
And the Chevisaunce,
Shall match with the fayre flowre Delice."

(Coronations=carnations; Sops-in-wine=striped pinks; Pawnce=pansy; Chevisaunce=wallflower; flowre Delice=iris.)

At this time we were still great flesh-eaters, and vegetables and herbs were used only for seasoning and sauces to give flavour to the meat. But fruit was appreciated for its own sake, and Tusser, that versatile man, in 1573 made a list of fruits to be planted (or removed) in January, which shows what was being grown at that date. Pippins—so called because they were grown from seed instead of by grafting—were introduced in 1503, and so would figure among Tusser's "apple-trees of all sorts." Then there were

"apricocks (still rare), barberies, boollesse (bullace), cheries, chestnuts, cornet plums, damsens, filbeards, goose berries (newly introduced along with raspberries), grapes, plums, hurtillberries (whortleberries), medlars, mulberie, peaches (still inferior), peares of all sorts, perare plums (pear-plums), quince-trees."

Besides herbs for healing, other plants were cultivated by the good housewife for use in cookery. Tansy, elderflower, cowslip, dandelion, borage, marigold, violet, rose and primrose were among the plants used in tasty dishes or in cordials and syrups. Sugar was a luxury known only to the wealthy; therefore sweetness in puddings and cakes had to be obtained by other means. Flowers were pressed into service, and honey was used—in fact, the bee-garden with its hives was a feature of some gardens; but even so, the sweetmeats of the Tudors were less sweet than ours, and this may explain their fondness for fruit.

There were some notable lesser gardens in London during this period. Many of the Livery Companies were already long-established—though more were to be created in the next century—and charming gardens surrounded some of the Halls. A garden and forecourt composed the street-front of the Tylers and Bricklayers Hall; the Brewers had a pretty little enclosure; and the Barbers cultivated herbs and simples in their physic garden. Pewterers' Hall stood in a lovely garden with a bowling green of which the Company was proud, and a vinery that yielded an abundance of grapes. The little walled garden of the Girdlers, in Basinghall Street, also boasted a vine as well as a mulberry tree and a fine leaden cistern. This was one of the two surviving Companies' Gardens until the last war, but on December 29th, 1940, it was destroyed by enemy action, and now forms part of that desolate acreage of exposed and weed-grown cellars behind Guildhall and stretching away to Cripplegate.

The other remaining garden was that of the Drapers' Company. Originally this was a rather small piece of ground belonging to Thomas Cromwell, Secretary of State to Henry VIII; and how Cromwell enlarged it in high-handed fashion is told by Stow, who naturally had some personal feeling about the matter:

"This house" (Cromwell's) "being finished, and having some reasonable plot of ground left for a garden, hee caused the pales of the gardens adjoining to the north part thereof, on a sudden to be taken downe, 22 foot to be measured forth right into the north of every man's ground, a line then to be drawn, a trench to be cast, a foundation laid, and an high bricke wall to be builded. My father had a garden there, and there was a house standing close to his south pale; this house they loosed from the ground, and bare upon Rowlers into my Father's garden 22 foot ere my Father heard thereof."

And because at that time Thomas Cromwell was all-powerful, "No man durst goe to argue the matter, but each man lost his land."

After its owner's execution in 1540 the Drapers' Company acquired the property, and until Victorian days it provided a welcome breathing space for the City. At one time a mulberry orchard reached as far as London Wall, and one of these old trees still remains among younger ones in the garden as a pathetic reminder of those spacious days. When Lord Macaulay was a child his parents lived near-by in Birchin Lane, and the little boy was often taken to play in the Drapers' Garden. After he grew up he always cherished an affection for this spot. Much of the ground has been built over, but a small rectangular enclosure remains, pleasantly laid out with shrubs and flowers and trees, and having in the centre a fountain. It forms, in Throgmorton Avenue, one of those oases of verdure and quietness that one comes across so often in the City. When the Drapers give a ball the garden is illuminated, and takes on a romantic aspect.

Crosby Hall, in Bishopsgate, where Sir Thomas More lived for a time, had a garden, and so had the mansion of Sir Thomas Gresham in the same thoroughfare. A fine garden at Bethnal Green belonged to Sir Hugh Plat. Among his contemporaries he was known for his knowledge of everything to do with gardening; but to-day he is remembered chiefly for his fascinating book, *Delightes for Ladies to Adorn their Persons, Tables, Closets and Distillatories with Bewties, banquets, perfumes and Waters.* It was published in 1602, and its recipes seem to perfume the air as one reads them: there are candied rosemary flowers, distilled waters of thyme, lavender and rosemary, sweet and delicate pomanders, washing balls, conserve of red damask roses, cowslip and violet vinegars, marigolds candied in wedges Spanish fashion, candied nutmegs . . .

The citizens of London found their gardens useful at the time of the Great Fire in 1666. Pepys tells us that on the 2nd September he "did by moonshine, it being brave, dry, and moonshine, and warm weather, carry much of my goods into the garden . . ." and on the 4th September,

"Sir W. Batten not knowing how to remove his wine, did dig a pit in the garden, and laid it in there; and I took the opportunity of laying all the papers of my office that I could not otherwise dispose of. And in the evening Sir W. Pen and I did dig another, and put our wine in it; and I my parmazan cheese, as well as my wine and some other things."

During the Fire we find him "sitting melancholy with Sir W. Pen in our garden"; and at night "walking into the garden" (he) "saw how horribly the sky looks, all on fire in the night."

At the end of the seventeenth century Gibson reviews very briefly some contemporary gardens in London: the names mentioned of private individuals convey nothing to us to-day, but Sir Henry Capel's garden at Kew stirs a memory, and we visit it later. The Queen Dowager (Mary of Modena) had a garden at Hammersmith, "my Lord Ranelagh's Garden" was but newly made, there were gardens at Beddington House and Arlington House.

There were also many important nursery gardens, and experiments were being made in forcing vegetables and fruit to save the difficulty of procuring them from abroad when they were out of season here. Richard Bradley, who wrote a great deal on Botany, Natural History and Gardening, tells us about some of these gardens in 1706:

"The first which are Kitchen Gardens and exceed all the other gardens in Europe for wholesome produce variety of Herbs are those at the Neat-Houses near Tuttle (Tothill) Fields, Westminster, which abound in Salads, early Cucumbers, Colliflowers, Melons, Winter Asparagus, and almost every Herb fitting the Table; and I think there is no where so good a school for a Kitchen gardener as this place; tho' Battersea affords the largest natural Asparagus and the earliest Cabbages. Again, the Gardens about Hammersmith are as famous for Strawberries, Rasberries, Currants, Gooseberries, and such like; and if early Fruit is our Desire Mr. Millet's at North End, near the same Place, affords us Cherries, Apricocks, and Curiosities of those kinds, some months before the Natural Season."

Chelsea abounded in market gardens and orchards; and there were many other nurseries in other parts of London, as we shall find. The changing fashions in gardening could not affect the citizens' gardens to any great extent: the new landscape style was as useless for small plots as had been the Italian and French—one could not have vistas and avenues and lakes in a piece of ground the size of a cabbage-patch. Only the Dutch fashion could be adapted for the use of Londoners, and no doubt they availed themselves of trees in tubs, clipped shrubs, gravel and grass walks, trimmed hedges and other features. Or they may have ignored any change of style, and just cultivated their plots as they liked. One thing is certain—Londoners retained their gardens at any cost. Thomas Fairchild, in *The City Gardener*, 1722, says:

"I find that most persons whose business requires them to be constantly in town will have something of a garden at any rate. One may guess the general love my fellow citizens have of gardening, in furnishing their rooms and chambers with basons of flowers and Bough pots, rather than not have something of a garden before them."

More than this: as far back as 1603 window-boxes had come into fashion.

Fairchild made a special study of trees and plants suitable for London, as "everything will not prosper . . . because of the smoke of the sea-coal." But in spite of this disadvantage he made surprising discoveries in various parts of the City; a vine was bearing good grapes in Leicester Fields; there were figs in Cripplegate and Chancery Lane, lilies of the valley in an enclosure behind Guildhall, pear trees in narrow alleys near Aldersgate, Bishopsgate and Barbican. In fact, he came to the conclusion that almost anything would grow in London if given proper care. And we can agree with him when we see trees that were formerly

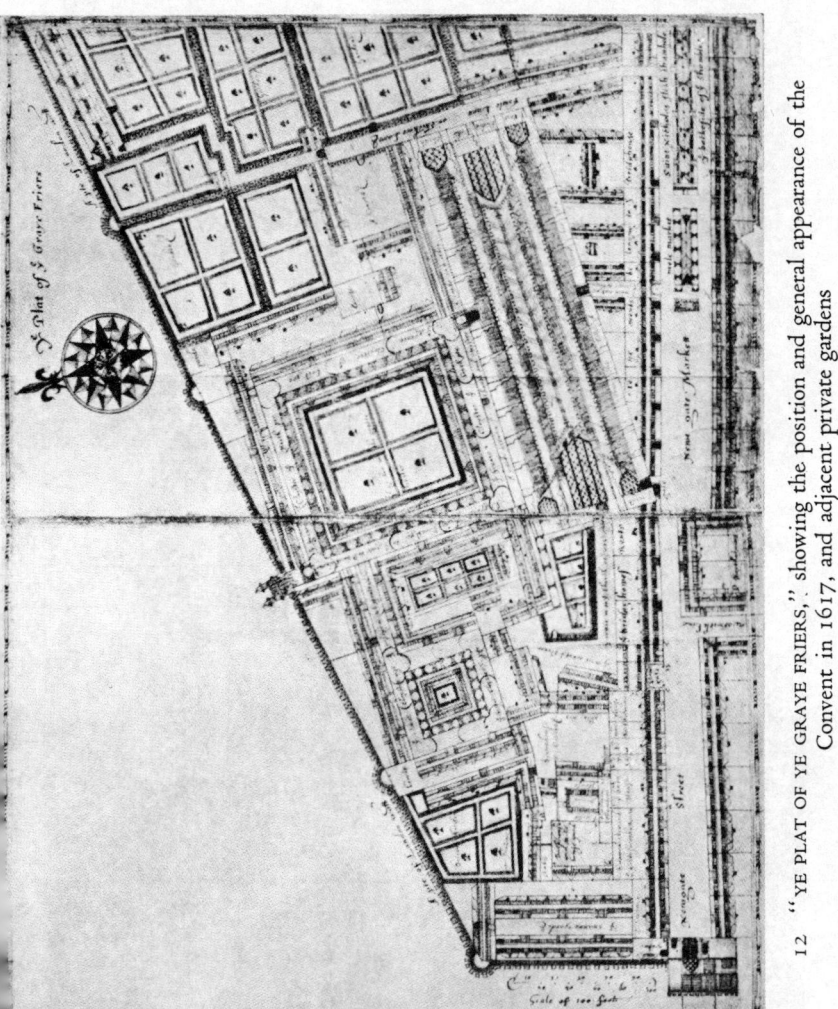

12 "YE PLAT OF YE GRAYE FRIERS," showing the position and general appearance of the Convent in 1617, and adjacent private gardens

75

13   A formal Town Garden of 1614, showing flower-beds, arbours and galleries

76

considered exotic, such as catalpa, ailanthus and acacias, flourishing in various districts, figs ripening at Lambeth, and pomegranates at Chelsea.

As London continued to expand, the City and its purlieus were increasingly given over to business, and the citizens moved farther and farther out to live. But some remained in the heart of the metropolis, and good old Thomas Fairchild would smile with pleasure to see how Londoners have remained true to their garden-loving tradition. In 1938 no less than 1,611 small gardens in the Metropolitan Police area were judged in the final All London Garden Championship.

To-day the London County Council holds garden competitions twice a year, in spring and summer, among residents on its cottage estates and among groups of "pre-fab" bungalows. Front gardens are judged, and awards made for flowers, shrubs, turf, etc.; and for dwellers in blocks of flats there are window-box competitions.

Then there is the work of the Women's Voluntary Services, which often co-operates with the London County Council. Since the last war they have sponsored a Garden Gift Scheme whereby various London boroughs have been "adopted" by certain counties, and benefactors in these counties supply seeds and plants for gardens of the "pre-fab" houses. Gifts of seeds have also been received from America. More than 20,000 little gardens in London are included in this scheme, and among flowers grown are fuchsia, lobelia, saxifrage, polyanthus, carnation, montbretia. pentstemon, spiraea, as well as pyrus, escallonia and deciduous shrubs. There is great competition in flower-growing between the boroughs, and for some years before her death Queen Mary presented a cup for the best garden; other prizes are given for lawns and various garden features.

Fifty years ago the late Lord Noel-Buxton and a group of enthusiasts founded the London Gardens Guild to encourage the cultivation of flowers in window-boxes in drab and congested districts. This work has been greatly extended, and is now carried on by the London Gardens Society which aims at "making a permanent contribution towards the beautification of London by the growing of flowers," especially in dull and ugly areas. Appropriately, the Society's badge is a sprig of London Pride; and it keeps in touch with architects and town-planners for the purpose of securing space for gardens in and around public buildings and private houses that are to be erected.

To this Society are affiliated many gardening societies in the metropolis, and competitions are held and prizes awarded for front and back gardens, large and small, window-boxes and balcony displays, gardens round "pre-fab" bungalows and on bombed sites. Schools take part as well as private individuals, and special prizes are given for the best shows in crowded or industrial areas The gardens are quite astonishing in their wealth of flowers and tasteful displays: one would never believe that such beauty could be achieved in districts such as Stepney, Deptford, Bermondsey, Bethnal Green, Lambeth, Paddington, St. Pancras, etc.

The Queen-Mother is Patron of the Society, and her Majesty takes great interest in the work, frequently visiting the gardens in different parts of London. In the year 1948–9 more than 10,000 gardens were judged, and no less than 70 silver cups as well as medals and certificates were distributed. The winners included schoolchildren, residents of L.C.C. estates, officers of the Metropolitan Police and members of London Guilds.

And so we see that Londoners are still great garden-lovers. The golden thread of continuity is being spun before our eyes, for citizens going home to their gardens in early summer will find that they have borrowed something from every period of history—mediaeval lilies, irises, columbines and peonies; lilac, laburnum, pansies and sweet-williams of Elizabeth's time; tulips reminding them of the seventeenth-century craze for those flowers, auriculas or bears' ears of the same period, to quote only a few examples. All ages come together in these gardens: they are a glorious inheritance. And in their turn the citizens are continuing to make history, for every garden is a reflection and a record of personal taste and character.

CHAPTER VI

Hampton Court

H AMPTON COURT is an epitome of English gardening. Here we can trace Tudor, French, Italian and Dutch styles as they succeeded each other in all their charm and contrasting beauty. And when we tire of horticultural fashions we can relax and let our minds wander to the people who have lived here. Few gardens are more saturated with personal associations: here Wolsey, Henry VIII, Elizabeth, William and Mary, Anne and the Georges all dropped their high estate and became men and women like ourselves, musing or making love, walking or driving, chatting, gardening, doing needlework in their gardens.

We first hear of Hampton Court in the days of the Knights Hospitallers of St. John of Jerusalem, who had a house and garden on this site. Then in 1514 Prior Docwra and his brethren leased the Manor of Hampton to "Thomas Wulcy, Archbisshop of York" for 99 years at a rental of £50 per annum. The estate consisted of 2,000 acres (chiefly pasture land) out of which Wolsey made Bushey Park and the Home Park. The gardens were like those of any other monastic establishment, with orchards, fish-ponds, a hare-warren and so forth. One sole relic of the Knights still exists: it is the bell of the clock in Clock Court that strikes the hours. It probably hung in the Chapel of the Order and was rung for their services, and the inscription it bears is + STELLA+ MARIS + MARIS+ SUCCVRRE+ PIISIMA+ NOBIS+ (Mary most holy Star of the Sea, come to our aid).

Wolsey threw a moat round his house and gardens although there was no longer any need for defence. The gardens were probably walled, and certainly held many of the turfed seats, arbours and alleys still popular at this time, and a knot garden; and on fine evenings the Cardinal-Archbishop walked there with his chaplain and said his Office. His royal master walked there, too, often with an arm flung round the prelate's shoulder in a characteristic gesture. Few traces of Wolsey's garden now remain: his knot garden was first replaced by Henry's Cloister Green Court, and then demolished to make room for Fountain Court and the State Apartments of Wren. The remainder of his gardens stretched across the present Pond Garden; and sightseers dawdle where the great Cardinal was wont to pace and meditate upon imperial politics. But peaceful Fountain Court still brings him to mind in

> "My garden sweet, enclosed with walles strong
> Embanked with benches to sytt and take my rest,
> The Knots so enknotted it cannot be espres't,
> With arbors and alyes so pleasant and so dulce
> The pestylent ayers with flowers to repulse."
>
> (Crawford)

The present knot garden on the south side of the Palace is a modern reproduction based on patterns published in the reigns of Elizabeth and James I, and was designed by Sir Ernest Law, the historian of Hampton Court Palace. The box-edged beds are crammed with the mauve and silver-green of lavender and the brighter silver foliage of southernwood, and in hot summer the air is filled with the humming of bees and the idle fluttering of butterflies above the massed herbs. As the heavy scent of lavender and lad's love is wafted from the beds one's mind can travel back and back and back . . . to the red-robed Cardinal musing in the quiet garden he loved.

In 1529, after Wolsey's banishment, Henry VIII took possession of Hampton Court, and at once began to alter and improve the gardens. The main idea was to arrange them to suit our changeable climate: to have dry walks, walled parterres, sheltered alleys, cloisters and summer-houses for wet and cold weather; and for the summer to lay out grassy plots, shady nooks, flowery bowers, banqueting houses and arbours. At this time Henry was young, handsome, cultured, active and fond of sport. To provide exercise he made a tilt yard, seven acres in extent, where joustings were held amidst great splendour of banners and tapestries. There were five towers for spectators, as well as a gallery in the north-west angle of the Palace, and stables for the horses of the knights and esquires. To-day one tower remains and forms part of the tea-rooms; and the tilt yard, which William III turned into a kitchen garden, is partly garden, partly car-park and partly sports ground.

Bowling alleys and "tenys plays," both outdoor and indoor, were also laid out by Henry; and Wolsey's parks were stocked with deer and other game so that the King could indulge in his favourite sport of hunting. Changes were made in the pleasure gardens, too. There was a flower garden to supply the Queen with roses; an orchard full of medlars, apples, cherries, damsons, melons and cucumbers; and a kitchen garden planted with herbs. The Hampton Court accounts are very human documents: as we read the entries we can almost see the gardeners busily at work, deciding where the new trees must go, and then planting them out:

"200 young treys of oke and elme, five score to every hundryth, at 12s. 6d. the hundryth, to sett in the Kynge's Great Orchard" . . . "Appultres and Pere-tres for the Kynge's new Orchard at 6d. the pece; 5 Servys treys at 14d. the pece; 4 holyff trees (holly) at 3d. the pece" . . . "Small sets of woodbyne and thorne, at 5d. the hundrythe" . . . "Treys of Yow, Sypers, Genaper (juniper), and Bayes at 2d. the pece" . . . "600 chery trees at 6d. the hundred."

In 1533 the gardens were partly re-made, and divided up by brick walls. From this year dated the King's New Garden, on the site of the present Privy Garden. This was laid out with gravel paths and little raised mounds having sundials on them. There were sixteen in all, and the accounts attribute them "To Bryce Augustyne, of Westminster, clokemaker for makyng of 16 brasin dyalles serving for the Kynges new garden at 4s. 4d. the pece."

Below the walls of the garden fruit trees were set in beds of flowers which were rather limited in variety at that time; we note "100 roses at 4d. the hundred, Violettes and Primroses . . . Gilliver-slips, mynts and other sweet flowers: Sweetwilliams at 3d. the bushell." Railed flower-beds were set in the grass; and in spite of the lack of flowers the general effect of these must have been charming. Over the rails roses were trained, and in the middle of each bed was planted a little tree of juniper, cypress or yew. The railings were striped in the Tudor colours of green and white (green symbolizing eternity, white purity); and at intervals were set posts bearing heraldic beasts of carved wood, painted and gilded and holding shields or vanes. These railings and beasts can be seen in the background of the Holbein picture in the Palace, repre-senting Henry and his family—but the garden depicted there is actually that at Whitehall.

These curious animal shapes figure in the accounts. There are pay-ments "for making of bestes in timber for the king's new garden," and for "the queen's bestes"; payments to "joiners setting up the bestes upon the posts in the privy orchard." And some idea of the variety and number of the creatures can be gained from an entry in 1534 for gilding and painting ". . 11 harts, 13 lions, 16 greyhounds, 10 hinds, 17 dragons, 9 bulls, 13 antelopes, 15 griffins, 12 leberdes (leopards), 11 yallys" (curious creatures, half boar, half goat), "9 rams, and the lion on top of the mount, also the vanes."

These fantastic "beestes" must have imparted an air of indescribable gaiety to the Palace gardens. To-day we see them sitting aloft along the roof of Henry's Great Hall, their gilded vanes swinging in the breeze and gleaming in sunshine; and they grin a cheerful welcome from stone columns bordering the Moat. So absurd and irrepressible they are—lions, unicorns, griffins, horses, leopards and the rest, grasping their shields in impossible attitudes. What must their splendour have been when, in gold and brilliant colours, they graced also the Pond Yard and the Mount!

The Pond Yard seems to have held only ponds and beasts—and perhaps sundials, for these occurred plentifully everywhere, One stone pedestal for a beast still remains in a corner of the garden wall. In Henry's time the water was supplied by "labourers ladyng of water out of ye Temmes to fyll the ponds in the night tymes." When the gardens were dark and deserted, and the sombre battlemented pile of the Palace showed only a few twinkling lights, a string of yokels carrying "pots and dishes" would straggle from the Pond Yard to the riverside and back again, to and fro endlessly, till with the aid of these small receptacles the ponds brimmed again. One hopes that this night-shift was paid adequately: "Weders in the Kynges New Garden and the Mount" earned 3d. a day, and "women weding" only 2d.; "Watering of the flowers" was paid for "at like price."

The Mount, to which reference has been made, stood at the southern end of the King's new garden. It was a great artificial mound built up of 256,000 bricks covered with earth, planted with quickset, and surmounted by an elaborate three-storied summer-house. To reach this building one climbed by winding paths bordered with more heraldic beasts, of stone this time, painted in their heraldic colours and bearing vanes: they stood on stone bases. Round the foot of the Mount was planted "a border of rosemary 3 years olde." The summer-house was also called the "Great Round Arbour" or the "Lantern Arbour."

Each storey consisted chiefly of glass, and the roof was a leaden cupola topped by a crowned beast carrying a large vane.

Summer-houses, banqueting-houses and galleries were usual in Tudor gardens, and at Hampton Court there were many turrets and towers in the grounds on the south side, towards the river (14). All were connected by galleries of wooden poles and trellis work that were probably covered with creepers or roses, vines or honeysuckle. On the river-bank stood a large tower flanked by turrets and having a water-gate and stairs; and here the King used to disembark when he came by barge to the Palace. A private corridor, "The Water Gallery," led from this tower to the arbour on the Mount, which in its turn was connected by another gallery to the Palace, and thus his Majesty could proceed in dry comfort from the river to his apartments.

Fertile orchards and the tilt yard with its five towers, flower-beds and striped railings, ponds and sundials, galleries, summer-houses and the Mount—and, thickly scattered, those fantastic beasts that vied in brilliance with the gaily-clad courtiers and ladies who flitted hither and thither. The magnificence of the Tudor age was expressed in the gardens of Hampton Court; and through the splendid scene moved the dominating and flamboyant figure of the King who planned it. This place has known grim tragedy, but it has also witnessed happiness, though sometimes of only a transient nature. One likes to remember that here the handsome "bluff King Hal" disported himself with his "awne darling," Anne Boleyn; and here, later, the disillusioned monarch sought to recapture youthful happiness in his brief love for Katherine Howard, the "dazzling rose without a thorn."

Anne has her memorial here in the "pleached alley" of wych elm, commonly and erroneously known as "Queen Mary's Bower." Records prove that its date is earlier than Mary's time, and that it was originally known as "Queen Anne (Boleyn)'s Bower." Of that alley Evelyn wrote: "The cradle-walk of horn-beam" (but it is wych elm) "is, for the perplexed twining of the trees, very observable."

The Tudor gardens have long since been stripped of their richness and decoration; they have been re-arranged and laid out afresh more than once. And yet, in spite of their comparative bareness, the atmosphere of those days persists to a remarkable degree, and one wonders if the ghost of poor Katherine Howard, shrieking in the Haunted Gallery, ever finds solace in the gardens below.

After the death of Henry VIII the splendour of the great Palace and its grounds was dimmed until Elizabeth came to the throne, and held her court there. She had a great liking for the gardens, and had them well tended. When staying at Hampton Court she would take a brisk walk in the grounds every morning about eight o'clock, "to catch her a heate in the colde mornings." Hunting and shooting parties and revels revived the former magnificence, and the Queen used to meet her advisers in the arbours of the garden. The aspect of the grounds remained pretty much the same as in her father's reign. Visitors remarked on the "sundry towers, or rather bowers for places of recreation and solace and for sundry other uses," at various points in the gardens; they also noted "the rosemary so nailed and planted to the walls as to cover them entirely, which is a manner exceeding common in England," and the gardens "laid out with various other plants, which are trained, intertwined and trimmed in so wonderful a manner, and in such extraordinary shapes, that the like could not easily be found."

But there was actually little change in the property. Although in the reign of Charles I Italian influence showed itself in terraces, loggias, fountains and pergolas, statues and garden ornaments in the great gardens of England, Hampton Court was hardly affected. A few fountains and statues replaced some of Henry VIII's vanes: otherwise the grounds remained unaltered until the reign of Charles II.

This monarch was fond of gardening. He knew the magnificence of great gardens in France with their superb vistas, elaborate fountains, immense parterres, terraces, flights of steps and statues, and brought with him from exile the latest French ideas, which found expression in his alterations at Hampton Court. To him we owe the laying out of the Home Park in almost its present form; the planting of the great avenues of limes round a semicircular parterre and radiating from the centre of the East front of the Palace (15); the digging of the long canal, which, with its border of trees, would remind him of his stay in Holland. How different was this spacious scheme from the intimate, enclosed gardens of Tudor times!

The plans for the formal lay-out were French in design (but not by Le Nôtre as some have supposed); and the work was carried out under the superintendence of John Rose, the King's gardener. A special messenger was sent to Holland to bring back 4,000 lime trees for the avenues. Besides the central fountain in the parterre before the East

14 HAMPTON COURT PALACE IN 1538: Showing the gardens with their railings and "beestes" on posts; also
the galleries connecting various towers, and the mount

From a drawing by Antonius Wyngaard

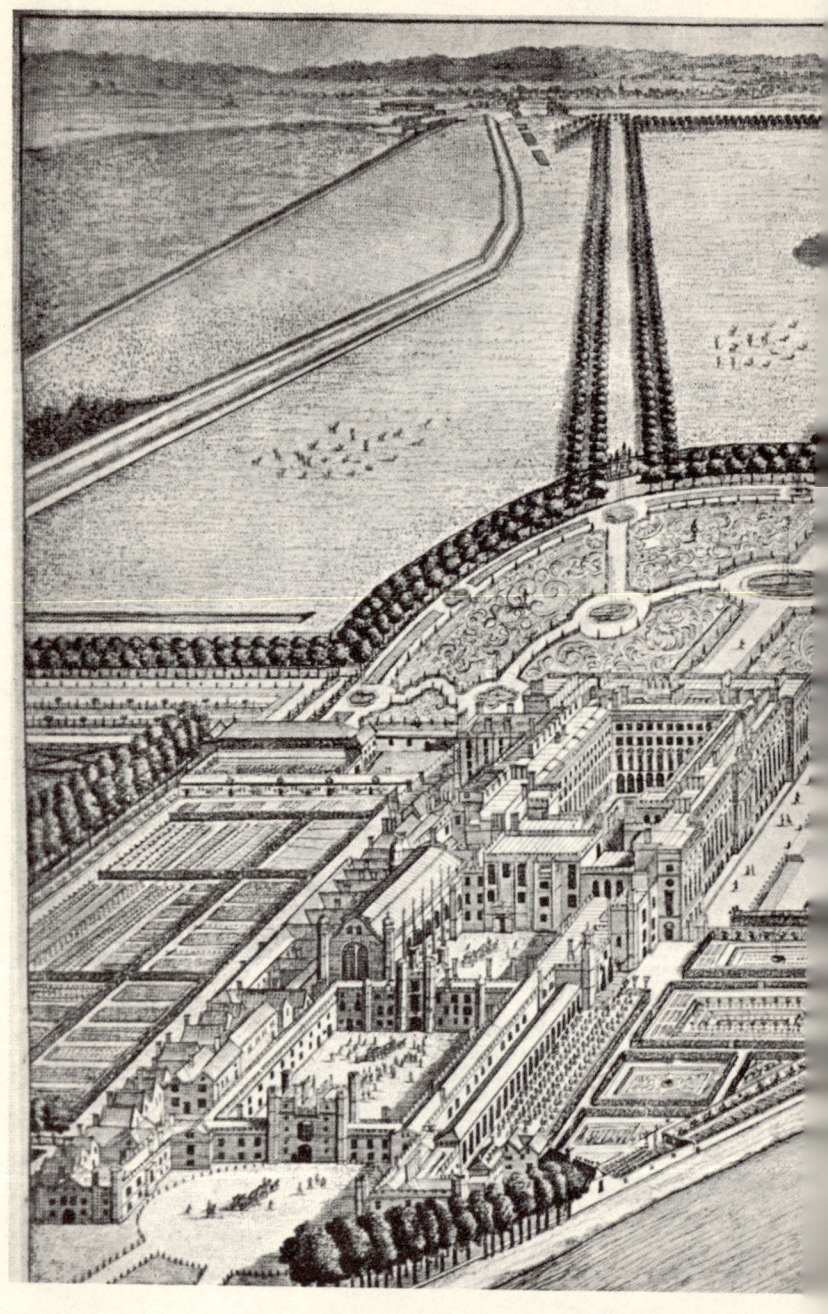

15   HAMPTON COURT PALACE: A bird's-eye v
From an engravin

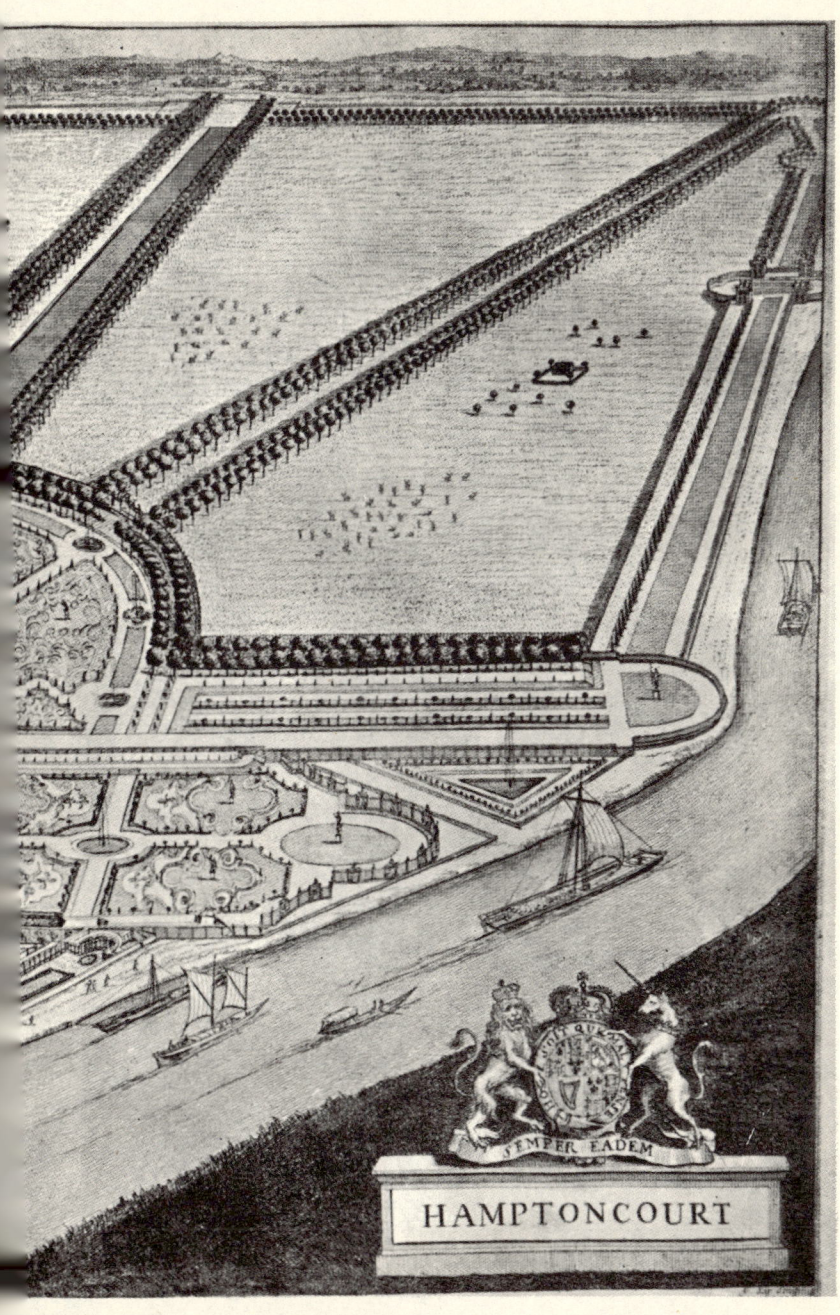

HAMPTONCOURT

about 1720, with the Thames in the foreground
Kip, after L. Knyff

16   HAMPTON COURT PALACE: The twelve Fountains set in the Parterre
From an engraving by I. Harris, after M. A. Hondmoy, c. 1720

front, there were twelve smaller fountains in imitation of Versailles, plots of grass, and geometrical beds with a clipped, cone-shaped, dwarf yew tree in the middle of each (16). Some of these yews still exist. Evelyn was rather critical of the alterations:

"The park formerly a flat naked piece of ground now planted with sweete rows of lime trees; and the canalls for water were perfected; also the hare park. In the garden is a rich and noble fountaine, with syrens, statues, etc. by Fanelli, but no plenty of water. . . . There is a Parterre which they call Paradise, in which is a pretty banquetting house, set over a cave or cellar. All these gardens might be exceedingly improved, as being too narrow for such a place."

A side-light is shed on this "banquetting house" (probably the old Water Gallery) by Hentzner, a German traveller. He described it in 1598 as "a certain cabinet called *Paradise* where besides that everything glitters so with silver, gold and jewels as to dazzle one's eyes, there is a musical instrument made all of glass except the strings."

William III was enchanted with Hampton Court. Its flat country, its long, straight, tree-fringed canal were reminiscent of his native Holland, and its seclusion and nearness to London made it just the kind of place he wanted as a home. Besides, the air agreed with him. Both he and Mary were garden-lovers; and while the new State Apartments were being built to Wren's design, and William was frequently away in London, Mary had the Water Gallery fitted up and decorated for her use, and lived there, taking a practical interest in the laying-out of the grounds and personally superintending the gardeners. (The Water Gallery was demolished in 1700, after her death.)

We can trace the influence of Bishop Compton at Hampton Court, for the Queen sent to Virginia and the Canary Islands for rare and exotic plants, and grew many from seed in the hot-houses established in the Privy Garden, and in the old Melon Ground which was that part of the old Kitchen Garden lying between the Tennis Court Lane and the old Moat. Another link with Compton was the fact that the Royal gardener at this time, George London, had formerly been gardener at Fulham Palace.

As might be expected, orange trees figured in Mary's gardening. They had been introduced into this country at the time of the Restoration, but some of the trees at Hampton Court were brought over from William's garden at Het Loo, in Holland. They were grown in tubs or square boxes which could be moved about; and as long as the State Apartments remained unfinished Mary stored her trees during the winter in the cloisters of the new quadrangle. During the summer the tubs stood along the walk on the South side of the State Apartments.

Under William's guidance former French features of the gardens became merged in the Dutch style. The taste of the Netherlanders ran to clipped yews and trees in pots, beds of flowers and plants elaborately designed like lace patterns, arbours, leaden statues, the clever use of water in fountains and —in their own country—little canals.

At Hampton Court the large fountain was removed from the parterre to Bushey Park (where it still stands), and the number of smaller fountains was increased in the great semicircular garden on the South side of the Palace. Some of the lime trees bordering this parterre were taken up and replanted in a more southerly position—a great feat, for they were more than thirty years old. The Broad Walk, nearly half a mile long, was designed, but there was no glorious herbaceous border such as we see to-day. Instead, on the other side of the walk there stretched the new parterre laid out in patterns of scroll-work outlined with box, and the scrolls filled with coloured sand. Stephen Switzer, who worked under William's gardeners, London and Wise, remarked of this, ". . . the only fault was the pleasure gardens being stuffed too thick with box, a fashion brought over by the Dutch gardeners who used it to a fault, especially in England where we abound in so good grass and gravel." Queen Anne's first work was to uproot this box because, it was said, she hated the smell.

While all these alterations were being carried out, what happened to the delightful Tudor gardens on the other side of the Palace ? Were they left alone ? No, indeed. William and Mary levelled the Mount at a cost of £500, because it spoilt the view of the river from the State Apartments. They remodelled the Privy Garden, and sunk the ground there 10 ft. to improve the view still further. They also laid out the Pond Garden in small enclosures with tall hedges to shelter the new exotic plants. (But it has since been restored to something like its Tudor appearance.) The present Banqueting House was built in 1700 on the site of one of the many Tudor towers that existed along the riverside. An arbour was made at the end of the pleached alley, and there Mary, that practical Queen, used to sit with her ladies and sew.

The tilt yard was divided into six kitchen gardens having high brick walls against which fruit could be trained; and the Old Orchard was converted into a very tame "Wilderness" with tall clipped hedges that excluded light and air, and straight regular walks. It existed like this till 1743; and in the centre was an espaliered labyrinth known as Troy Town. Later this was transformed into a rockery.

Dutch gardens were well known for their mazes, so it was only natural that William should construct one at Hampton Court. In shape it is a triangle, and the length of the sides is 230 ft., 107 ft. and 91 ft. respectively. Although the area of the maze is less than an acre, the winding paths amount to half a mile in length. The hedges were originally of hornbeam, cypress and flowering shrubs, but they have since been patched with holly, hawthorn, privet and sycamore.

Ornamental grilles or *clairvoyées* were another expression of Dutch taste: in small gardens they gave the illusion of vistas. And for this purpose Jean Tijou, perhaps the most famous worker in iron, designed twelve screens to surround the Private Gardens. They were made in 1694, and Sir Ernest Law does not exaggerate when he describes them as "the finest specimens of decorative ironwork ever executed in England, and it is doubtful whether this metal has ever, in any country or any age, been moulded into forms more exquisitely delicate and graceful." After being moved about a good deal, the screens have been returned to the riverside end of the Privy Garden, where one can examine every lovely detail of festoons, national emblems—rose, harp or thistle—and the royal monogram, "W.M."

Anne did not do much for the gardens. Pope, in *The Rape of the Lock*, gives us a glimpse of her at Hampton Court (p. 93):

> "Close by those Meads, for ever crownéd with Flow'rs
> Where Thames with Pride surveys his rising Tow'rs
> There stands a Structure of Majestic Fame,
> Which from the neighb'ring Hampton takes its Name.
> Here Britain's Statesmen oft the Fall foredoom
> Of foreign Tyrants, and of Nymphs at home;
> Here Thou, great Anna! whom three Realms obey,
> Dost sometimes Counsel take—and sometimes Tea."

The Queen was much addicted to driving about the grounds, backwards and forwards, in and out of the avenues for about 20 miles at a time—20 miles of comparative dullness, one would think—and for this purpose had the roadways levelled and the holes in them filled in. Like her predecessor, she was a practical woman, and used to sit in the gardens with her ladies-in-waiting and do needlework. But, except for having the box edges to the flower-beds removed, she did nothing to make or mar the grounds.

George I used to retire from London and his much-disliked subjects to Hampton Court. He considered it a convenient spot where he might live undisturbed with his two ugly German mistresses after whom was named the Frau or Frog Walk under the wall of the tilt yard, near the Palace gate. There these ladies used to go to meet the King when he returned from London.

A few changes were made in the grounds about 1736, for Queen Caroline took up gardening with William Kent, and together they substituted large, plain lawns for the scroll-work beds and numerous fountains in the great parterre. Luckily these alterations were only superficial, and did not interfere with the general plan of the grounds. The Broad Walk at this time was bordered by long, narrow beds containing tall, pyramidal yews and short, rounded holly trees; these made an agreeable edging to the new and spacious lawns.

With George III's accession in 1760 Hampton Court ceased to be a royal residence, and, except for the State Rooms, was gradually divided up into suites of apartments which were allotted by the grace and favour of the Sovereign to private families. The grounds remained under the supervision of "Capability" Brown, at that time Royal gardener of Hampton Court. The King asked him to "improve" the gardens and adapt them to modern fashions; but for once Brown was wise, and declined the task "out of respect to himself and his profession." We shall be for ever thankful to him for this decision which helped to preserve the past for us.

It was probably Brown who planted in 1769, in a corner of the old Pond Garden, the Great Vine. This belongs to the Black Hamburgh variety, which has small ovate berries, and was a slip from the vine at Valentine's, near Wanstead, Essex. In any case this kind of vine grows to an enormous size and is very prolific, but the extraordinary luxuriance of the specimen at Hampton Court is probably due to the fact that its roots have penetrated to the bed of the river, only 60 ft. away, and are therefore receiving the maximum of nourishment. In early days as many as 2,200 bunches of grapes were gathered, but the crop is now controlled and kept down to less than a third of that number.

By the nineteenth century the craze for landscape gardening was over, and flowers were beginning to come into their own again. After "carpet-bedding" came a reaction in favour of more natural planting. William Robinson was a pioneer of this movement, and he studied the blending of flowers so as to compose rich, harmonious masses, Surely he must have attained the highest expression of this idea in the wonderful herbaceous border which he laid out along the Broad Walk! This is one of the most splendid borders in England; its beauty changes as the plants are renewed and replaced, but never dies. Half a mile of flowers! Half a mile of form and colour and fragrance! It is the apotheosis of Hampton Court, the culmination of loveliness that we have followed through Tudor, Stuart and Hanoverian times—and free to all the world since Queen Victoria ordained it so in 1838.

17 *The Rape of the Lock*
From an engraving by Lud. du Guernier, 1714

CHAPTER VII

Famous Gardeners

Turner, Gerard, Parkinson, L'Obel, Tuggie,
the Tradescants, the Gardeners' Company

No book on London gardens would be complete without some
account of the men who helped to design them, worked in them,
were consulted by their patrons, and brought their skill, intelligence and patience to the service of the garden.

In early days horticulture and healing went hand in hand, and were
practised by the monks. They had the learning and practical experience,
they owned or wrote the precious manuscripts treating of the nature
and properties of herbs, medical instructions, garden lists, practical
directions for grafting and sowing, and also cookery books. These
gardeners of the mediaeval ages were chiefly anonymous, and the
information they have left behind is scrappy and sometimes unreliable.
But with the invention of printing gardening knowledge spread; and
after the Dissolution the sciences of botany and medicine (still closely
associated) passed into secular hands.

It is only when we reach the Tudor age that names and personalities
begin to emerge clearly. As might be expected, a period so rich in the
development of gardening produced the men needed for this expansion. The gardeners of this period were often herbalists, apothecaries,
botanists and writers rolled into one. The first of any note was Dr.
William Turner, "the Father of English Botany," whom we have
met at Syon House. He was a most versatile man—Doctor of Medicine,
Fellow of Pembroke Hall, Cambridge, Dean of Wells, botanist and
physician to Edward VI and the Protector Somerset; also a friend of
Latimer and Ridley. He was born between 1510 and 1515 at Morpeth,
in Northumberland, and after studying at Cambridge travelled in
Italy, Germany and Holland, and received his M.D. degree in Italy.

After his return to England he held several ecclesiastical appointments, and was made Dean of Wells; but when Mary came to the throne he was deprived of his Deanery, and had to go into retirement.

Like many other men, when the winds of fortune blew cold he turned to gardening as a solace. He lived at Kew and had a garden there, but was often at Syon, on the opposite bank of the river, where he laid out the old formal gardens: his *Names of Herbes* (1548) was dated from that house and dedicated to his patron, the Protector Somerset. In 1551 his *Herbal* was printed, and its second part followed in 1562. Previously, in 1538, he had written *Libellus de Re Herbaria*, and dedicated it to the King, Henry VIII.

From Turner we learn about the fruits introduced at this time: the raspberry was new, and "the taste of it soure": the gooseberry (planted in 1516 in some of Henry VIII's gardens) he calls "a groser bushe, a gooseberry bushe," and says, "It groweth only that I have sene in England in gardines, but I have sene it in Germany abrode in the fields amonge other bushes." The apricot or apricock (introduced about 1524, probably by Henry VIII's gardener, Wolf), was still a rarity. Turner writes that "it were better to cal it an hasty Peche tree, because it is lyke a peche and it is a great whyle rype before the pech trees. . . . But so that the tre be well known, I pase not greatly what name it is knowen by." A new and useful plant brought to this country by him was lucerne, which he called "horned clover."

On the accession of Elizabeth Turner was reinstated. He died in 1568, and was buried in St. Olave's, Hart Street, the church always associated with Pepys (and destroyed by bombing).*

Probably the best-known gardener and writer of this time is John Gerard. Everyone knows of, or has dipped into, his famous *Herbal*, which was written in 1597. It is not a very original book, being copied largely from other people's works, but it makes entertaining reading, and the woodcuts are a joy in their formal quaintness and accuracy (19).

Gerard was born in 1545, at Nantwich, in Cheshire. Someone has described him as "a rogue, but an engaging one." At any rate, he was a physician and also a practical gardener, and had a garden at Holborn, on the slope of the hill between Ely Place and the Fleet, a spot surrounded by woods, fields and meadows. In those days Holborn was a

* It is now being rebuilt (1953).

little country hamlet hardly big enough to be called a village, and stonecrop and flowers grew on the houses. In this place Gerard used to gather trefoil, yarrow, lesser hawkweed, red clary, white saxifrage and rocket; and in Gray's Inn shepherd's purse, mallow, bugle and sweet woodruff.

The herbalist's own garden contained about eleven hundred plants, many of them rarities such as the "Blew Pipe the later physicians do name Lilach," the laburnum and Judas tree. Some plants may have come from Lord Burghley's famous gardens at Theobald's Park, Hertfordshire, which was such an inspiration to Sir Francis Bacon, and from Cecil House in the Strand, for Gerard was in charge of both these gardens. And many more may, in the first instance, have come from abroad, for at that time horticulturists were obtaining plants and seeds from other countries. In 1579 Cecil received from a friend in Italy "fifty of the rarest seeds in Italy"; and the martagon or Turk's cap lily was sent to him with other rare bulbs from our Ambassador in Turkey.

Gerard himself used to send a collector to the Mediterranean regions, and amongst other spoils received plants of the prickly pear and seeds of the plane tree. We cannot help wondering if Shakespeare ever visited him, for between 1598 and 1604 the poet lived quite near, and his plays are so full of flowers and herb-lore that it seems more than likely he was acquainted with the great herbalist and his garden.

In 1596 was published the first complete catalogue of plants in any garden, a twenty-four page list of Gerard's own plants; and a year later came the great *Herbal* dedicated to Lord Burghley. This was revised in 1603 by Thomas Johnson, himself an eminent botanist, and this edition is generally considered more reliable than the first. Gerard was elected Master of the Barber-Surgeons' Company in 1607, and died in 1611. He was buried in St. Andrew's Church, Holborn, with no monument to mark his grave.

Contemporary with Gerard was John Parkinson, also an apothecary, who had a garden in Long Acre that was "well stocked with rarities" (18). Not much is known about his personal life beyond the fact that he was born in 1567, died in 1650, and was buried in St. Martin-in-the-Fields. He was Apothecary to James I, but his chief claim to fame is his *Paradisus*, or, to give the work its full and comprehensive title, "*Paradisus in sole Paradisus Terrestris; or a garden of all sorts of pleasant flowers,*

IOANNIS PARKINSONI PHARMACOPOEI LONDINENSIS EFFIGIES·LXII·AETATIS ANNVM AGENTIS·A·NATO·CHRISTO·CIƆƆCXXIX·

18   JOHN PARKINSON (1567–1650)
Reproduced from his "Paradisi in Sole," 1629

97

19 JOHN GERARD (1545–1612)
From an engraving by John Payne on the title page of the 1633 edition of "The Herball"

Iohannes Tradescantus Filius pene ingenue
paterni verus heres, relictum sibi rerum varus
congestarum thesurum ipse plurimum adavcet
et in Musæo Lambethano unicis virtudini exhibet.

W. Hollar ad vivem delin et sculp

20 JOHN TRADESCANT THE YOUNGER
(1608–62)
From an engraving by Wenceslaus Hollar

which our English ayre will permit to be nursed up; with a kitchen garden . . . and an orchard," etc. The book was dedicated to Queen Henrietta Maria, and the title was a pun on his own name—"Park-in-Sun's Earthly Paradise." Although the author was, like Gerard, accused of borrowing other people's writing, this great tome (published in 1629) is far more original in content, and for more than a hundred years was the most complete English dissertation on the subject: it is still one of the loveliest gardening books.

After its publication Charles I appointed the author "Britanicus Regius Primarius." The following year Parkinson brought out his *Theatrum Botanicum*, and dedicated it to the King as it was a more "man like Worke" than the *Paradisus*, which he considered feminine: it has more to do with botany than gardening.

Parkinson had no children, and perhaps for that reason lavished his affection on flowers. To dip into the *Paradisus* is to wander through a fragrant garden where every plant is beloved. Let us follow the owner and listen to his comments:

"What shall I say to the Queene of delight and of flowers, Carnations and Gilloflowers, whose bravery, variety, and sweete smell ioyned together, tyeth euery ones affection with great earnestnesse, both to like and to have them. . . . The Crowne Imperiall for his stately beautifulness, deserveth the first place in this our Garden of Delight, to be here entreated of before all other Lillies."

He finds "Yellow Larkespurre, the prettiest flower of a score in a garden," and says that "Hollihocks . . . yeeld out their flowers like Roses on their tall branches; like Trees, to sute you with flowers, when almost you have no other to grace out your garden."

He mentions Coventry Bells (*Campanula medium*) as well as Canterbury Bells, and gives lists of "English" (indigenous or long-established) as well as "out-landish" or imported blooms. How delightful are the names of Medowe Saffron, the "white and blew Syringa or Pipe tree," the Melancholick Gentleman (*Hesperis tristis*), Dames Violets (a gilloflower), Larkes heels or spurres on toes, Floramour or flower-gentles (*Amaranth purpurea*).

We could linger long with this dignified and gentle writer, and cull from his pages many "a delicate Tussiemussie, as they call it, or Nosegay, both for sight and sent." We could follow him while he gives us instructions for the care of grapes and vines, trees, roses and grafting, orchards and kitchen garden; but space will not allow. He shall give us a last message to this effect:

"That as many herbes and flowers with their fragrant sweet smels doe comfort and as it were revive the spirits and perfume a whole house: even so such men as live vertuously, labouring to doe good and to profit the Church of God and the Commonwealth by their paines or penne, doe as it were send forth a pleasing savour of sweet instructions, not only to that time wherein they live, and are fresh, but being drye, withered and dead, cease not in all after ages to doe as much or more."

At this time in London there was quite a fraternity of well-known gardeners: they were all on good terms, and it must have been stimulating to hear of and see each other's work during a period when new plants were being brought into the country, to compare notes and exchange seeds and plants.

Among this company was L'Obel, a Frenchman (born in 1538), who supervised the garden in Hackney belonging to Lord Zouche, another great patron of horticulture. L'Obel had travelled about Europe and practised medicine on the Continent before he came to England. James I appointed him "botanist to the King"; but he is best remembered as the man after whom the lobelia is named.

Then there was Ralph Tuggie who had a celebrated garden in Westminster. He was known especially for his carnations, pinks and auriculas, and some of them bore his name: there were "Master Tuggie, his Rose Gilliflower," and "Master Tuggie's Princesse." After his death, some time before 1633, the garden was kept up by his widow.

One of the most honourable names in the history of gardening is that of the Tradescants. There were three generations, all bearing the same name, but the third John Tradescant died at the age of nineteen: that leaves us with John Tradescant the elder, and his son, John Tradescant the younger. They were all buried in one tomb in old Lambeth churchyard.

The family may or may not have been of Dutch extraction. We first hear of the elder Tradescant in 1607, when he was in service to Robert Cecil, first Earl of Salisbury and Lord Treasurer of England. On behalf of his master Tradescant was sent abroad a good deal to bring home new varieties of fruit—mulberry, cherry and apricot—and flowers—tulips, martagon lilies, anemones, Provence roses and several kinds of irises, besides orange trees in pots, a pomegranate, oleanders and myrtles, peaches, muscat grapes and white figs. What enrichment for the Earl's garden! And in addition his gardener produced a black cherry notable for size and flavour, which was known as "Tradescant's Cherry," and the glorious double daffodil that Gerard called *Narcissus roseus Tradescanti*.

After Cecil's death in 1612 Tradescant worked for Lord Wotton at Canterbury (probably in what is now the garden of the Warden and Fellows of St. Augustine's Missionary College), and during this period availed himself of Captain Argall's expedition to Virginia for obtaining new plants for his garden. Among them was the little purple flowering rush, the spiderwort, so familiar in our gardens, to which Parkinson gave the name of "Tradescantia." In 1618 John the elder joined an expedition to Archangel, which gave him an opportunity of studying Russian flora; and in 1620 we find him travelling to Algiers, whence he brought back the "Argier Apricocke, yellow, sweet and delicate," and the "corn flagge of Constantinople," which was the gladiolus. Parkinson wrote truly of his friend that "He hath wonderfully laboured to obtain all the rarest fruits he can hear of in any place of Christendom, Turkey, yea, or the whole world."

In 1626 Lord Wotton died, but before that Tradescant had gone to George Villiers, Duke of Buckingham; then, thanks to the Duke's influence, he was appointed head gardener to Charles I. It was about this time that he went to live in Lambeth, and established his Physic Garden and "Cabinet of Rarities" known as "Tradescant's Ark," which was actually the first museum in this country. It was well patronized, for among the visitors were Charles I and his Queen, the Duke of Buckingham, the second Earl of Salisbury, Archbishop Laud and Sir Thomas Herbert, the Persian traveller.

The date of the elder Tradescant's death is unknown, but it was possibly 1637. He left everything to his son, John, who inherited his father's tastes and centred his life round the Physic Garden and the Ark. At the Restoration the extreme popularity of these exhibitions led to a warrant being issued for Tradescant's arrest for "making a shew of severall strainge creatures without authority of His Maiesties Office of the Revells." This was an absurd accusation, and Tradescant straightway appealed to the King, who not only gave permission but also a royal testimonial which ran: "Our express pleasure is that the said Tredeskyn be suffered freely and quietly to proceed as formerly in entertaining and receiving all persons whose curiosity shall invite them to the delight of seeing his rare and ingenious collection of Art and Nature."

"Rare and ingenious" the collection certainly was, for it included a Dodo, a Dragon Egg, a flea-chain of 300 links, and the knitted gloves of Edward the Confessor! But the catalogue of contents which Tradescant drew up with the aid of his friend, Elias Ashmole, also contained a most attractive list of flowers brought from foreign countries by the two gardeners and their friends. Among the plants were Virginia Ladyes Bower, Indian Sorrell, New England Strawberry, Orange Tawney Anemone of Constantinople, Dames Violets of Italy, a yellow Mallow of Tartary. In addition, the tulip tree and the deciduous cypress ranked among the novelties imported.

Tradescant the younger died in 1662. He left the Physic Garden and the "Cabinet of Rarities" to Elias Ashmole, who took no interest in plants. The Garden was neglected, and fell into oblivion, but the Ark eventually passed to the University of Oxford, and became the foundation of the Ashmolean Museum. It may seem rather unjust that the name of Ashmole should be thus perpetuated instead of Tradescant, the originator of the Ark: but Tradescant is immortalized in the flowers that bear his name—daffodils, spiderworts, Michaelmas daisies (*aster Tradescanti*)—and what lovelier commemoration could a man desire?

Ever since mediaeval times there had been market gardeners in London, and in James I's reign they, and others of such diverse occupations as botanists, greengrocers, florists, fruiterers, herbalists, foresters, garden-implement dealers, fruit growers and seedsmen, formed themselves into the Gardeners' Company, and obtained Royal Charters in 1606 and 1616. Their authority extended throughout the City and within a radius of six miles, and they controlled "the trade, crafte or misterie of gardening, planting, grafting, setting, sowing, cutting, arboring, rocking, mounting, covering, fencing and removing of plantes, herbes, seedes, fruites, trees, sticks, setts, and of contryving the conveyances to the same belonging." The Company was empowered to search for and destroy any unwholesome or rotten goods in the markets, and no one could set up as a gardener without their permission. There were special regulations for "foreigners"—the French and Flemish refugee gardeners, who were regarded with jealousy.

In spite of vicissitudes during the succeeding centuries the Gardeners' Company still survives, and ranks as sixty-sixth among the City Livery Companies. Long ago their functions ceased to be necessary: there was no scope for practical gardening in the City when Londoners moved out to the suburbs and cultivated their gardens there. The local retailer of garden produce was largely superseded by the wholesale merchant; plants, seeds and gardening necessities arrived from all over the world to be marketed in London; and scientific gardening made great strides. But the Company moved with the times and directed its energies into other and more modern channels. Scholarships have been awarded; a library of technical works on gardening has been established in the Guildhall Library; and the Gardeners are intent on advancing the interests of horticulture in every way possible.

Also in 1606 was established the "Masters, Wardens, and Commonalty of the Mystery of Fruiterers of London," whose duties were "the victualling and serving the citizens with good and wholesome fruit." Their work and that of the Gardeners seem to have overlapped in some respects; but the Fruiterers still remain among the City Livery Companies, and are forty-fifth in order of precedence.

CHAPTER VIII

Vanished Gardens

The Great More House
Sir William Temple's Gardens
Sayes Court

INSUBSTANTIAL as a dream, and anchored to reality only by fragments of old red brick walls, lies Sir Thomas More's beautiful garden, overlaid by the houses that crowd together in that part of Chelsea between Battersea Bridge and the King's Road. But let us ignore the streets and houses and the noisy traffic, and try to picture the well-loved home of that great and dauntless statesman, where he loved to retire from London and the Court, and enjoy his family life and literary pursuits.

Chelsea seems always to have been a place of gardens, and no wonder: salubrious air, real country, the river and a convenient distance from London made it popular, and even Henry VIII did not disdain to own a manor house there. The Earl of Shrewsbury had a mansion close by; later, the Earls of Lindsey and Sir Arthur Gorges owned notable houses and gardens on either side of Beaufort House, and Danvers House was also famed. But the finest of all the properties in the sixteenth century was that of Sir Thomas More: its position and its layout were unrivalled.

The Great More House, afterwards known as Beaufort House, stood where Beaufort Road runs into King's Road, and was described by Erasmus as "neither mean nor subject to envy yet magnificent and commodious enough." It was a long building from east to west, and the garden, which ran down to the river, extended as far as from Church Street on the east to Milmans Street on the west. Next to the house lay two large courtyards, and the remainder of the land was laid out in formal gardens and orchards, with stables on the present site of the

Moravian burial ground, and the farmhouse and barns on the site of Lindsey House, in Cheyne Walk.

North of the house the grounds extended to Fulham Road. The King's Road did not then exist: this, a narrow cart-way at first, was made for Charles II, who wanted a short cut from Whitehall to Hampton Court (where the gardens were being laid out in the new French style) to save going through the rowdy village of Knightsbridge and the mud of Hammersmith.

The earliest plan in existence is dated 1597, when the house had passed into the possession of Sir Robert Cecil. He was being so busy—and extravagant—over completing Hatfield at this time that he probably had not yet done much in the way of alteration to his Chelsea house; and so we can take the plan as a partial guide, at any rate (22). It shows a long terrace stretching eastwards from the house, with a door from which inside stairs led up to the chapel. Curious little lodges (definitely later than More's time) were set angle-wise between the two forecourts, and a broad avenue ran down from the house to the riverside, where there were landing stairs and a quay. There must have been a barge-house, too, for the eight-oared barge which Sir Thomas used for going to the City or Whitehall.

This was an ideal situation for a home. To-day Whistler's house stands on More's river-bank, and, remembering the wonderful effects of mist and sunshine which the artist painted, we can imagine how much lovelier it must have been four hundred years ago, when the Surrey side was pasture land and woods, and the Thames, far wider then, swept in a great shining curve from Fulham to Chelsea, and flowed on broadly to Westminster, unconfined by any embankment.

This, then, was the setting for Sir Thomas More's private life, for the family gatherings and entertainments of friends which he loved. He lived in simple style here. The household was large and patriarchal, and included his wife and his son, his three daughters and their husbands with eleven grandchildren; also his secretary and "a learned young kinsman." The portrait group by Holbein in the National Portrait Gallery shows Sir Thomas with some members of this family; and it delineates perfectly the thoughtful, wise and firm character in the countenance of the Chancellor.

His friends were legion. The King was a frequent visitor, sometimes arriving unexpectedly, sometimes spending whole days at Chelsea, and showing affection by throwing his arm around More's neck as they walked in the garden together. (But the Chancellor was wise enough to value this intimate gesture at its true worth.) It was said that Henry bought Chelsea Manor after discovering the salubrity of the air at the Great More House. And he considered the climate so healthy that he made the Manor a residence for his young daughter, Elizabeth, then three or four years old.

More was the first patron of Holbein, and the painter was often at Chelsea. Erasmus and Dean Colet, Tunstall, Linacre and John Heywood, the playwright, all went there, and Heywood has left us his impression of the garden: "Wonderfully charming, both from the advantage of its site . . . and also for its own beauty; it was crowned with almost perpetual verdure; it had flowering shrubs, and the branches of fruit trees interwoven in so beautiful a manner that it appeared like a tapestry woven by Nature herself." This is practically the only contemporary comment that we have; but More may have had his own home in mind when he wrote, in *Utopia*, "We all went to my house, and entering into the garden, sat down on a green bank and entertained one another."

There must have been good talk at the great house, for Sir Thomas was keenly devoted to the new learning, and the most distinguished men of the day, foreign as well as English, sought him out. Erasmus described More's home as

"a university of the Christian religion, for though there is none therein but readeth or studieth the liberal sciences, their special care is piety and virtue; none seem idle; that worthy gentleman doth not govern with proud and lofty words, but with well-timed and courteous benevolence; everybody performeth his duty, yet there is always alacrity; neither is sober mirth wanting."

In 1532, when he found it impossible to maintain his position in view of the separation of the Church of England from Rome, More resigned the Chancellorship and retired to Chelsea, where he spent the next two years quietly with his family. Was it during this time, one wonders, that he wrote of his garden:

"As for Rosmarine" (rosemary) "I lett it run alle over my garden walls, not onlie because my bees love it, but because 'tis the herb sacred to remembrance, and therefore to friendship; whence a sprig of it hath a dumb language that maketh it the chosen emblem of our funeral wakes and in our buriall grounds."

The garden witnessed his last, sad leave-taking of his home when he was summoned to Lambeth for his trial in 1534. He had been expecting this call: he had spent the night in prayer, and "earlie in the morning was housled, and for other matters had little care." Contrary to his usual custom, he would not allow his wife and children to accompany him to the riverside, but bade them farewell in the garden, closed the wicket gate behind him, and took boat for Lambeth. At first he sat "with a heavie hart, verie sadd," deep in troubled thought. Then suddenly he roused himself and said to Master Roper and the servants who were accompanying him, "I thank our Lorde the field is wonne."

After the trial (during which we caught a glimpse of him at Lambeth) he was committed to the Tower, and the next year was beheaded. His head was retrieved from a spike on Tower Hill by his daughter, Margaret Roper, and taken to Canterbury. It is now carefully kept in the little church of St. Dunstan, opposite her old home. His body rests in the More chapel of Old Chelsea church, which was the only part of the church to escape destruction during the Blitz.

As for the Great More House and its garden: after the execution of Sir Thomas it was sometimes used as a residence for royalty. Anne of Cleves died there in 1557, and Katherine Parr, after Henry VIII's death and her subsequent marriage to Admiral Seymour, lived there and had charge of the thirteen-year old Princess Elizabeth. Afterwards the estate passed through various hands, including Lord Burleigh, the Earl of Beaufort and Sir Hans Sloane. In 1625 the northern part of the garden was walled in and called Chelsea Park. This survived until the present century, and a writer has described a glimpse through its old iron gates of "a park of cedars, old mulberry trees, elms and whitethorn, full of blossom in the spring, all set in the long grass—more like the country than any London suburb."

The house was demolished in 1752, during Sir Hans Sloane's ownership, and traces of the garden are few and difficult to locate amidst the bricks and mortar of to-day. But Elm Park Gardens, Mulberry Walk, The Vale and Park Walk remind one of the former Park, on which they are built; and actual fragments of a wall belonging to More's farmhouse and barns can be seen behind Lindsey House in Cheyne Walk and at the back of the east side of Paultons Square. Part of the redbrick wall of his stables remains and forms part of a wall of the old Moravian burial ground, which is now a secluded and private spot simply and beautifully laid out as an expanse of green edged with a low box hedge and overhung by tall, shady trees.

That is all that remains of the famous home of a very great man. The aged mulberry tree on the Embankment, often associated with More, probably stood in the garden, but not in his time: mulberries were not introduced into this country until after his death. And a lovely gateway which we shall find at Chiswick House belonged to Beaufort House after More's time.

* * * *

The names of three distinguished garden-lovers stand out in the history of horticulture during the seventeenth century. One of them, Sir Francis Bacon, had no garden of his own in which to test his theories (although he was responsible for the gardens at Gray's Inn at one time), and so, although he writes charmingly he is apt to be unpractical in his ideas. The other two, Sir William Temple and John Evelyn, made their own gardens, and put so much knowledge, skill and practical experience into them that they became famous.

Sir William Temple's first garden was situated at Sheen, and his house was one of several erected on the estate of a former Carthusian monastery, the second conventual establishment founded by Henry V as an act of expiation. This and Syon House are referred to by Shakespeare in *Henry V* when he makes the King say:

> ". . . and I have built
> Two chantries, where the sad and solemn priests
> Sing still for Richard's soul."

The monastery at Sheen was a huge place: the buildings alone had a frontage of 3,000 ft., and the quadrangle was 300 ft. long by 100 ft. wide. Before the Dissolution the monks incurred Henry VIII's displeasure by supporting the cause of the Holy Maid of Kent; and probably foreseeing the course of events, they judged it more expedient to surrender their property to the King than to wait for its confiscation. The Priory buildings were given to the Earl of Hertford, and after his disgrace to the Duke of Suffolk, the father of Lady Jane Grey. Some historians say that she was married here to Lord Guildford Dudley in the presence of Edward VI: we know that after the ceremony she went to Syon House.

In Mary's reign the monastery and its monks were temporarily restored; and then it changed hands pretty frequently, and by the time of the Commonwealth was in a ruined condition. Some houses were built on the property, including the residence of Sir William Temple, where he was often visited by Charles II and James II. When Evelyn saw the Abbey in 1678 there was "yet remaining one of the solitary cells with a crosse."

Dates are contradictory, accounts of Temple's two gardens—at Sheen and afterwards at Moor Park, in Surrey—are confusing, and show historical discrepancies which may be due to the great diplomatist's frequent absences abroad. But Sir William carried out the same horticultural ideas in both gardens, so that the confusion does not matter much. In any case, we only get a series of vignettes, nothing tangible is left from which we can reconstruct the gardens. And what we remember to-day is not the lay-out of his grounds but what he accomplished in fruit- and vine-growing.

The property at Sheen was not very large, especially when compared with the tendency of the day to make gardens more and more extensive. Probably its area was that which Sir William had in mind when he wrote, "As to the size of the garden which will perhaps in time grow extravagant among us, I think from 4 or 5 to 7 acres is as much as any gentleman need design."

His own garden was laid out in the Dutch fashion. Temple would have seen and admired this at the Hague when he was our Ambassador to Holland. He played an important part in bringing about the marriage of William of Orange and the Princess Mary, Charles II's niece, and this union helped to spread the popularity of Dutch gardening style over here.

For flowers Temple had not much use, and wrote: "I will not enter upon any account of flowers, having only pleased myself with seeing or smelling them, and not troubled myself with the care, which is more the ladies' part than the man's." That sounds rather as though he left the flowers in the garden to the care of his wife, Dorothy Osborne; and it is quite likely that she undertook "the ladies' part," for she shared her husband's enthusiasm for gardening, and once wrote of a neighbour of hers in Bedfordshire: "But of late I know not how Sir Sam has grown so kind as to send to me for some things he desired out of this garden, and withal made the offer of what was in his, which I had reason to take for a high favour, for he is a nice florist."

Sir William specialized in the cultivation of fruit trees, and was particularly fond of his cherries, "Sheen plums," peaches and "standard apricocks." We get a good idea of this in his long essay, The Gardens of Epicurus (1685), where he tells us:

"I may truly say that the French who have eaten my peaches and grapes at Shene, in no very ill year, have generally concluded that the last are as good as any they have eaten in France, on this side Fountainbleau; and the first as good as any they eat in Gascony. . . . Italians have agreed, my white figs to be as good as any of that sort in Italy. . . . My orange trees are as large as any I saw when I was young in France, except those of Fountainbleau . . . as laden with flowers as any can well be, as full of fruit as I suffer or desire them, and as well tasted as are commonly brought over, except the best sorts of Spain and Portugal."

Evelyn wrote of the garden at Sheen in 1688: "The most remarkable things are his orangery and gardens, where the wall-fruit trees are most exquisitely nail'd and train'd, far better than I ever noted." Temple himself believed there were great possibilities for fruit-growing in this country:

". . . perhaps few countries are before us; either in the Elegance of our Gardens; or in the number of our plants, and I believe none equals us in the Variety of Fruits which may be justly called good; and from the earliest Cherry and Strawberry to the last Apples and Pears, may furnish every Day of the circling year."

And so he set himself assiduously to improve the quantity and variety of fruit produced in England. We may never know how much we are indebted in this respect to the great diplomatist.

He was also keenly interested in viticulture, and introduced no less than four new sorts of grapes into England. At that time they were still grown out of doors but not as extensively as in former days: in Elizabeth's reign vineyards were of great importance, and the vines were trained to poles and rafters. Why then was there this decline ? Sir Hugh Platt ascribed it to the "blockish ignorance of our people who do most unjustly lay their wrongful accusations upon the soil"; but Parkinson was probably right when he blamed the Dissolution—and the change in our climate. The monks had been skilful growers of vines, and those brethren coming from the Continent had brought with them the newest varieties and the latest improvements in methods of cultivation.

Though Sir William's gardens were derived in style from Holland, his grapes came from France, and the new varieties were the Arboyse, "a small white grape . . . the most delicious of all grapes that are not muscat"; the Burgundy, which he grew upon an east wall, and described as "a grizelin, or pale red, and of all others surest to ripen in our climate"; a black Muscat called the Dowager, that ripened as successfully as the common white grape; and the Grizelin Frontignac, "the noblest of all grapes I ever ate in England, but it requires the hottest wall and the sharpest gravel, and must be favoured by the summer too, to be very good." He adds, "All these are, I suppose, by this time pretty common among some gardeners in my neighbourhood, "as well as several persons of quality . . ."—which reminds us that The Vineyard, in Richmond, commemorates this growing of grapes in Sheen. In contrast to many people who possessed horticultural treasures and were jealous of their rarity, Temple distributed his vines generously, writing: "I ever thought of all things of this kind the commoner they are made the better."

When the revolution came Sir William remained neutral; and then he transferred his loyalty to the new King, William III, who would have made him Secretary of State, had he not resolutely declined to take office. After the death of his eldest son the family retired to Moor Park, near Farnham, where Temple passed the rest of his life.

Shortly after their departure Gibson visited Sheen, and has left us this account of it:

"Sir William Temple, being lately gone to live at his house in Farnham, his garden and greenhouse at West Sheene, where he lived of late years, are not so well kept as they have been, many of his orange trees and other greens, being given to Sir John Temple, his brother, at East Sheen, and other gentlemen; but his greens that are remaining (being as good a stock as most greenhouses have) are very fresh and thriving, the room they stand in suiting well with them, and being well contrived, if it be no defect in it that the floor is a foot at least within the ground, as is also the floor of his dwelling house. He had attempted to have orange trees to grow in the ground . . . and for that purpose had enclosed a square of 10 ft. wide, with a low brick wall, and sheltered them with wood, but they would not do. His orange trees in summer stand not in any particular square or enclosure, under some shelter, as most others do, but are disposed in pedestals of Portland stone, at equal distance, on a board over against a south wall, where is his best fruit, and fairest walk."

Temple's home at Moor Park was named after his favourite garden at

Moor Park, Hertfordshire, belonging to the Countess of Bedford. This he described as "the perfectest figure of a garden I ever saw." It had terraces, flights of steps leading down to parterres, gravel walks and fountains, statues, standard laurels, and was further elaborated by cloisters. Quite possibly the second Moor Park was modelled on the first (21).

Of the statesman's later home it was said:

"The air agreed with him, the soil was fruitful and well suited to an experimental farmer and gardener. The grounds were laid out with the angular regularity which Sir William had admired in the flower-beds of Haarlem and The Hague. A beautiful rivulet flowing from the hills of Surrey bounded the domain. But a straight canal which, bordered by a terrace, intersected the garden, was probably more admired by the lovers of the picturesque in that age."

William III used often to visit Sir William at Moor Park, and if his host was laid up with gout, as sometimes happened, Temple's secretary, Jonathan Swift, would escort the King round the garden. It is said that on one of these occasions his Majesty offered to make Swift his Master of the Horse, and in addition taught him to cut asparagus in the Dutch manner. At Moor Park Swift met his "Stella," and here began the great romance, for Hester Johnson was also of the household, acting as waiting-maid to Lady Gifford, Temple's sister, who lived with him.

In his will Sir William left the lease of certain lands in Ireland to Hester, "Servant to my sister Giffard," and £100 to Swift, to whom he had been a good patron for ten years. But the most touching clause in the will (after desiring that his body may be interred in Westminster Abbey) runs: "And I desire and appoint that my heart may be interred six foot underground on the South East side of the stone dyal in my little garden at Moreparke." This request was duly carried out.

Traces of this garden still survive, for Moor Park is now an Anglican Training College for Adult Education, and Temple's old house forms the core of the present mansion. Part of the canal that once bordered Sir William's parterres can be seen, as well as the long terrace walk and the foundations of a banqueting house and gazebo.

*   *   *   *

Deptford to-day is a thickly populated artisan district, a region of docks and dockyards. During the last war one part near the river was heavily bombed, and if you go there and turn off Evelyn Street you will find in the midst of devastation a pleasant garden that has been re-made since the war. It is a place where the aged can sit quietly among trees and flower-beds and lawns, and the young can play games, paddle or go on swings; a place of rest and recreation. And it is a precious spot: this little recreation ground is all that remains of the hundred acres of Sayes Court, the house and famous garden of John Evelyn, gentleman, diarist and garden lover of the seventeenth century. The rest has been swallowed up in streets and houses; and where the grounds formerly descended to the river there is now a long block of buildings.

Evelyn was born in 1620, at Dorking, and was educated at Balliol. He was a Royalist, but during the Commonwealth he managed to live undisturbed, chiefly occupying himself with his garden at Sayes Court. In contrast with Bacon, who was full of theories and experiments, Evelyn was a practical gardener, and did much to further horticulture in this country. But he was a courtier as well, and after the Restoration we find him on very good terms with Charles II, and occupying impor-tant positions at Whitehall. He had a wide circle of friends, and was one of the first members of the Royal Society. From his diary, which covers a period of seventy years, we learn much of the history of that time, and catch glimpses of his own and other people's gardens. The diary is an illuminating document, and as fascinating to read as that of Pepys.

Evelyn's other writings deal with various aspects of horticulture. *Sylva*, which he compiled for Charles II, is about forest trees. At that time there was a scarcity of timber because during the Civil War trees had been ruthlessly sacrificed; and now wood was badly needed for ships. By means of this book landowners were persuaded to take care of their woods "which the greedy rebels had wasted and made havoc of"; and very much later it was said—by Disraeli—that from the oaks which Evelyn caused to be planted were built the ships in which Nelson fought.

Evelyn tried to popularize the trees mentioned in *Sylva*: many of them, like horse-chestnut and plane, were still rare, and others such as larch, cedar and tulip tree were difficult to obtain. In 1664 he noted with regard to cedars that he had received "cones and seeds from the mts. of Lebanon"; and later he sent to America for plants and seeds of larch, lime, walnut, sumach, firs and other trees.

Another work, *Acetaria: a Discourse of Sallets*, contained recipes for salads, using the herbs of that time. *Kalendarium Hortense*, or *Gardener's Almanac*, was a popular book that indicated the flowers to be planted and the work to be done each month. Evelyn translated into English *The Compleat Gardener*, a French work that had much to do with the drying, pickling and preserving of fruit; and he also wrote a practical *Direction for his Gardener*, and a book with the long-winded title of *Fumifugium; or the inconvenience of the Aer and Smoak of London dissipated, together with some remedies*. This advised the planting of fragrant flowers in the suburbs. He gave long lists of plants, and pointed out that with the air "perpetually fanned" from so many sweet-scented shrubs and flowers, "the whole City would be sensible of the sweet and ravishing varieties of the perfumes." An idyllic idea, and greatly to be preferred to the fumes of petrol that hang about our streets to-day!

The purchase of Sayes Court was finally completed in 1653. According to a contemporary account, the property comprised a

"manor house built with timber, with the appurtenances, thereunto belongeinge commonly called Sayes Court, Deptford . . . consisteinge of one hall, one plor" (parlour?), "one kitchen, one buttery, one larder, wᵗʰ a daryehouse, alsoe one chamber and thre cellᵉʳˢ. In yᵉ second storie eight chambers, with foure clossets, and three garretts, two stables, and one other little stable joyninge to the aforesaid manoʳ house, which aforesaid manoʳ house together with the said garden orchard and courtyards conteine together two acres, two roodes, and sixteen pches."

Evelyn also purchased some adjoining land, and for that and Sayes Court paid £3,500. The name of the estate was derived from the family of Say, who had owned it in the twelfth century. By the time of James I it had reverted to the Crown, and was leased to the Brownes, who were Essex folk. Evelyn married a Miss Mary Browne of this family; and after they had lived at Sayes Court for some time, and she had succeeded to the property, he purchased the freehold from Charles II.

During 1653 Evelyn commenced the great task of making his garden. In January of that year he wrote:

"I began to set out the oval garden at Sayes Court, which was before a rude orchard, and all the rest one entire field of a hundred acres, without any hedge except the hither holly-hedge joining to the bank of the mount walk. This was the beginning of all succeeding gardens, walks, groves, enclosures and plantations there."

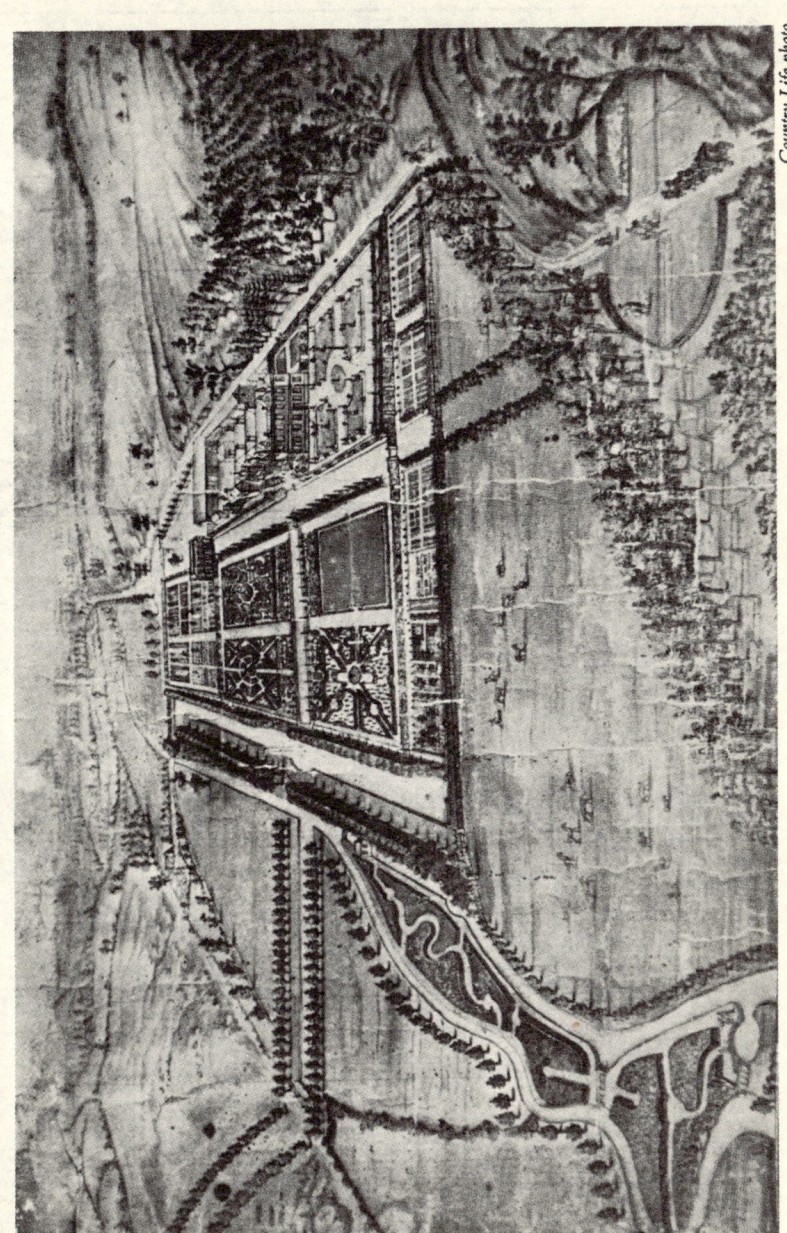

Country Life photo

21 MOOR PARK, Farnham, Surrey. A contemporary bird's-eye view of the lay-out of Sir William Temple's Garden

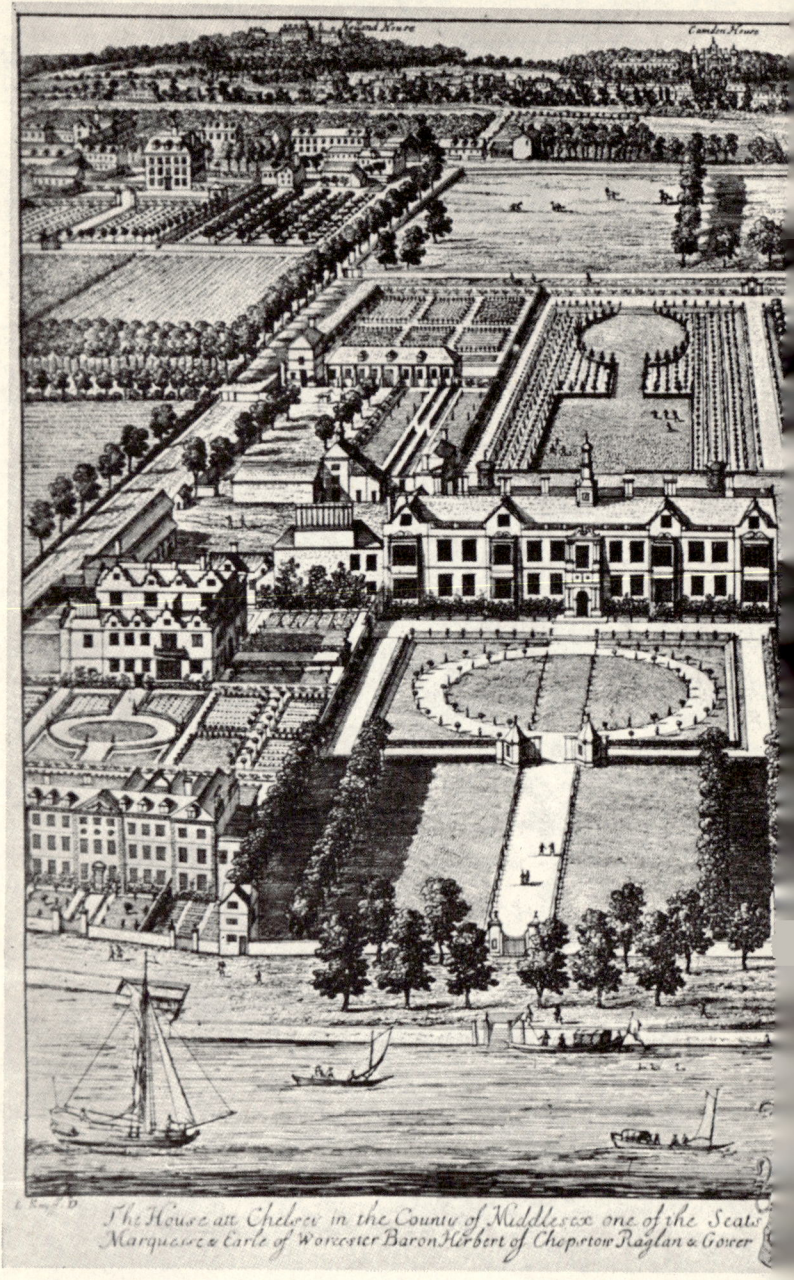

The House att Chelsea in the County of Middlesex one of the Seats
Marqueise & Earle of Worcester Baron Herbert of Chepstow Raglan & Gower

22 BEAUFORT HOUSE, CHELSEA, and its garden, about 1707. Originally "The G
    was when Sir Thomas More lived th
                                        From an engraving

Kingsinton House

of the Most Noble & Potent Prince Henry Duke of Beaufort
and Knight of the Most Noble order of the Garter.

J. Kip Sca.

e House," this is (except for the two little lodges in the forecourt) just as it
the left is Lindsey House (c. 1674)
ip, after L. Knyff, 1707

23   CHELSEA HOSPITAL in the late seventeenth century: Showing the twin canals before their "arms" were added

From an engraving by B. Cole

As we read on in the diary we see the garden taking further shape. March 4th, 1664: "Planted the Home Field and West Field about Sayes Court with elms, being the same year that the elms were planted by His Majesty in Greenwich Park." In December of that year: "I planted the lower grove next the pond at Sayes Court. It was now exceeding cold and a hard long frosty season, and the Comet was very visible."

The gentlemen of the Restoration were keenly interested in the cultivation of bulbs, especially tulips, which were known as "onions," and commanded high prices. John Evelyn did not indulge in this craze as much as his friends, but he used to exchange seeds with them and import plants from abroad. We find one of his intimates, Sir Thomas Hanmer, a noted horticulturist, writing to him in 1671:

"I send you herewith some rootes of severall sorts: the bear's ears" (Auriculas) "and some of the anemones and ranunculus are very good, but the tulips . . . are not extraordinary . . . I suppose your flower garden, being new, is not very large, and therefore I send you not many things at this tyme, and I wish the beares ears doe not dry too much before you receave them."

On February 4th, 1684, the diary records: "I went to Sayes Court to see how the frost had dealt with my garden, where I found many of the greens and rare plants utterly destroyed. The oranges and myrtles very sick, the rosemary and laurels dead to all appearance, but the cypress likely to endure it."

It is interesting to look at the garden and its owner through the eyes of other people. Pepys visited Sayes Court, and wrote: "Then to Mr. Evelyn's, to discourse of our confounded business of prisoners, and sick and wounded seamen, wherein he and I are so much put out of order. And here he showed me his gardens, which, for variety of evergreens, and hedge of holly, the finest things I ever saw in my life. Thence in his coach to Greenwich, and there to my office, all the way having fine discourse of trees and the nature of vegetables." Pepys also notes that "among other rarities" Evelyn had "a hive of bees so as being hived in glass you may see the bees making their honey and combs mighty pleasantly."

A little later (Feb. 1665–6) we come across a personal impression:

"Up, and to the office; where among other businesses Mr. Evelyn's proposition about publick Infirmarys was read and agreed on, he being there; and at noon I took him home to dinner, being desirous of keeping my acquaintance with him; and a most excellent humoured man I still find him, and mighty knowing."

A critical light is shed on Sayes Court by Gibson in *A Short Account of Several Gardens near London* (1691):

"Mr. Evelyn has a pleasant villa at Deptford, a fine garden for walks and hedges (especially his holly one, which he writes of in his Sylva), and a pretty little greenhouse with an indifferent stock in it. In his garden he has four large round philareas, smooth clipped, raised on a single stalk from the ground, a fashion now much used. Part of his garden is very woody and shady for walking; but his garden, not being walled, has little of the best fruit."

We must go back some years for the beginning of the holly hedge which was to become renowned. A brief entry in Evelyn's diary for May 1st, 1683, says: "I planted all the out-limites of the garden and long walks with holly." He had a strong *penchant* for hedges of holly, and constantly exhorted his friends to plant them. His finest specimen at Sayes Court (planted still earlier, in 1670) was truly remarkable, being 400 ft. long, 9 ft. high and 5 ft. in diameter; and in *Sylva* he rhapsodizes:

"Is there under heaven a more glorious and refreshing object of the kind than an impregnable Hedge . . . which I can show in my poor garden at any time of the year, glittering with its armed and varnish'd leaves? the taller standards at orderly distances, blushing with their natural Corall. It mocks at the rudest assaults of the Weather, Beasts and Hedgebreakers."

But not at the systematized assaults of man, unfortunately. In 1698 the Czar of Russia, afterwards Peter the Great, came to England to learn ship-building, and rented Sayes Court from Admiral (then Captain) Benbow, to whom Evelyn had let it. The behaviour of this monarch seems to have been somewhat eccentric: besides doing considerable wanton damage to the bowling-green, fruit trees and grass, he had himself trundled in a wheelbarrow right through the famous holly hedge as a favourite morning recreation. Afterwards Evelyn wrote sorrowfully of "my now ruined garden at Sayes Court (thanks to the Czar of Muscovy)." His diary for June 8th, 1698, records: "I went to Deptford to see how miserably the Czar had left my house after three months making it his Court. I got Sir Christr. Wren, the King's Surveyor, and

Mr. London, his gardener, to go and estimate the repairs, for which they allowed £150 in their report to the Lords of the Treasury." And among the repairs were listed three damaged wheelbarrows!

This disastrous visit is commemorated in Czar Street, which turns off Evelyn Street. And in the Presence Chamber at Kensington Palace hangs a portrait of this ill-mannered monarch, painted by Kneller. It shows a dark, vivacious youth in armour, with an ermine-lined cloak flung over one shoulder; an arrogant young man quite capable of destroying another person's property just for fun.

John Evelyn always spoke modestly of "my poor garden," but at Sayes Court he entertained Charles II and his Queen, the Lord Chancellor, the Earl of Clarendon, the Earl of St. Albans, Samuel Pepys, Sir Christopher Wren, Robert Boyle and a host of other friends. Besides cultivating his own garden he helped to design and lay out others—the family seat at Wotton, in Surrey, Albury, near Guildford, and Chelsea Hospital were examples. And all this in addition to his public and official work, his travels and visiting.

In 1694, after the marriage of his daughter (his wife being long dead) Evelyn retired to Wotton to spend the rest of his life there with his elder brother, George; and there the diarist died in 1706.

All the glories of his garden at Sayes Court have vanished; the last hollies died about twenty-five years ago. But if the wraith of their kindly, cultured owner ever walks abroad he will be happy to see the good and beneficial *use* that is being made of this last remnant of his garden, for, as Austin Dobson says, he was ever "a generous enthusiast for anything tending to the improvement of his race or country."

CHAPTER IX

Chelsea Gardens

The Royal Hospital—the Physic Garden

To many people the Royal Hospital is merely a synonym for the Chelsea Flower Show that annually displays the latest triumphs of horticulture in those grounds; an affair of crowds and catalogues and flowers upon flowers. On such an occasion one can hardly be conscious of the Hospital, for it hides its personality from this publicity. But come here on an ordinary day, say in October, when Wren's fine buildings are caught in sunshine that lights up the pale stone porticoes and colonnades, and mingles the red of the creepers with the dingy red of old brickwork so that the walls glow warmly above the vivid green of the terraces. *Then* one realizes how lovely the Hospital is, standing on its slight eminence and overlooking the avenues of bronzed and golden trees and the river flowing mistily below. It must have been even lovelier in its early days, before the gardens were shorn of their richness.

The story of the Hospital goes back to the seventeenth century. After the Civil War the problem of maimed, sick and ageing soldiers became acute: there were so many of them, and no organization existed for their relief. Before the Reformation they had been largely cared for by monasteries and charitable endowments; but now these no longer existed, and "maymed souldiers" roamed the country, only occasionally receiving parish relief. Various plans to help them were put on foot with little or no success; and finally the formation of a regular army in Charles II's reign made definite action necessary, and the Royal Hospital was the result.

It seems a pity to kill a pretty story, but we are forced to confess that Nell Gwynn had nothing to do with the founding of this institution. John Evelyn was at that time responsible for the prisoners of war lodged at the Theological College, founded by James I in 1610, which stood on the site of the present Hospital; and Evelyn, Sir Stephen Fox (Paymaster of the Army) and Sir Christopher Wren launched a scheme for the needs of invalid soldiers, thus carrying out the King's wishes. Evelyn's diary for September 14th, 1681, records:

"Din'd with Sir Stephen Fox, who propos'd to me the purchasing of Chelsey Coll, which his Majesty had some time since given to our Society" (the Royal Society), "and would now purchase it againe to build an Hospital or Infirmary for Souldiers there, in which he desired my assistance as one of the Council of the R. Society."

By the next year the scheme was well in hand. Evelyn had been in frequent consultation with Sir Stephen Fox, and in the latter's study the two men drew up a list of the staff that would be required, and their salaries—the governor, chaplain, steward, housekeeper, chirurgeon, cook, butler, gardener, porter. And Evelyn had a kindly and unusual thought for the veterans: "I would needes have a Library, and mention'd several bookes, since some souldiers might possibly be studious when they were at leisure to recollect."

The foundation stone was laid in 1682, but it was not until 1692 that the Hospital was opened. Wren's original idea for the gardens was simply that they should consist of several walled enclosures, including a kitchen garden, "Backe Courte and Buriall place"; also a terrace on the south side, and a walk down to a water-gate on the river bank.

But the buildings had to be enlarged to take an increased number of pensioners, and so, in 1686, orders were given for the construction of two new quadrangles—Light Horse Court on the east and Infirmary Court on the west—and their flanking roads. The plan of the grounds, too, had to be revised. More land was acquired, and the gardens now formed an integral part of Wren's design, adding greatly to the dignity of the buildings.

Work on the gardens began in 1687, and lasted for five years. It was considered necessary to have a Great Court before the front, and so a space (now Burtons Court, and devoted to games) was "enclos'd, planted and made into Walks for the Diversion of the Soldiers." Avenues of lime trees and horse chestnuts divided the area into three parts corresponding to the three blocks of the Hospital, and a broad gravel walk ran the whole length of the north front. Hospital Road did not exist, so the Court stretched unbrokenly from the buildings. Royal

Avenue was designed at the same time as the Great Court, and later on
Queen Anne intended to make this a continuous avenue to go all the way
to Kensington. But owing to her death the project was never carried out.

We may wonder how Burtons Court got its name. Was it derived
from some military hero? Or some benefactor? From neither. There
was a certain James Button, a porter, appointed to that position in 1687.
His duties were multifarious, and kept him constantly before the public
eye: he had to be a combination of porter, butler, kitchen overseer,
beadle, policeman and general watch-dog. And for the better carrying
out of his tasks he was provided with an imposing and expensive livery
to wear. As a result of all this he considered himself a Personage, and
insisted on being treated as such. His very signature, a capital "B",
sprawled importantly across the pay-rolls. His special domain was the
Great Court, where he lived in one of the lodges for thirty years. It is
easy to see how his name came to be given, at first jokingly and then as
a matter of course, to the Court. To an illiterate man there would be no
difference between the spelling of "Button" and "Burton." But the
Great Court was often referred to locally as "College Fields."

On the east side of the Hospital Wren planned seven enclosures, all
the same length but differing in breadth. The northernmost was the
burial ground (in its present position); and if it is asked why this should
be so far away from the chapel, which was in the main building, the
answer is that Sir Christopher objected to graves in or near churches,
not only for sanitary reasons but because digging disturbed pavements
and foundations. Next came the narrow walled enclosure of the Physic
Garden, where fruit trees and "physical herbs" were grown until
1820; and adjacent to that a kitchen garden with espaliered fruit
trained against its high brick walls, and beds of "sweet herbs, sallads
and roots." Later, this was added to the Governor's Garden that lay
alongside it. An orchard came next, and then the gardener's service
yard with its greenhouse, sheds, and shelter for ladders; and lastly
the Paymaster-General's grounds that afterwards became Ranelagh
Gardens.

But of course the most impressive part of the gardens lay on the south
side of the buildings (23). A broad and imposing terrace extended the
full length of this front, and a magnificent vista was created, stretching
from Figure Court (where the statue of Charles II stands) down to the
river. This vista consisted of a wide, elevated causeway 80 ft. long

running between two straight, formal canals which in their turn were flanked by avenues of small trees and ditches. Two years later "arms" running east and west below the terrace were added to the canals, thus making them L-shaped (29).

In 1690 a long wharf was constructed, with stone stairs and a causeway out into the river; and the following year a couple of square summer-houses, simply furnished inside, were added at the ends of the wharf. The "Water Gardens" proved troublesome with regard to the proper circulation of water, and in addition two flat-bottomed boats were constantly in use to keep the canals free from weeds. But the fishing was good, and was preserved. (It must be remembered that there was a salmon fishery in Chelsea Reach.) In 1688 another canal, the Coal Creek, was dug on the western boundary of the grounds, so that barges could be unloaded there; and in 1760 what was probably the first avenue of plane trees was planted along the river bank between the wharf and the Coal Creek.

All the grounds were under the supervision of George London and Henry Wise, the royal gardeners, who went into partnership while they were working at Chelsea: the planting out here was probably their first important contract. This work began in 1688 and went on for eight years; but in 1691 the partners obtained a separate 10-year contract for the maintenance and cultivation of the gardens at a salary of £380 per annum.

The land on the south front of the Hospital did not consist entirely of pleasure grounds. Three and a half acres of meadow lay between the western canal and the Coal Creek, and this became the main kitchen garden. It was divided up by hedges and espalier screens of wood, and the list of vegetables grown there sheds light upon the diet of the day. The pensioners did not eat potatoes until 1816, but were nourished with onions, carrots, cabbage, celery and leeks: the staff enjoyed cucumbers (grown in a "melon ground"), cauliflowers, radishes, peas, spinach and beans. Pot-herbs were grown, and these could be infused by the pensioners "as tea, for their health or pleasure"; fruit was produced in abundance. This garden was given up in 1838, but the fruit trees stood till 1850.

The corresponding space to the east of the canals was afterwards arranged as a kitchen garden for Lord Ranelagh, but part was reserved as a bird sanctuary or, as it was quaintly put, "an island for fowles."

Unfortunately all this land was low-lying and apt to become flooded, even after the embankment was raised in 1783 at a cost of £1,840.

Looking at the grounds to-day, it is difficult to believe that they were ever laid out in such an elaborate manner, for hardly a trace remains. Under the influence of Victorian taste Wren's gardens vanished like a slowly dissolving scene in a film.

In 1845 Royal Hospital Road (at that time called Queen's Road) was cut across Burtons Court, and then a central avenue of trees was planted that spoiled the fine view of the main entrance and its lodges on either side. About 1850 the great south terrace was reduced to its present series of levels, and the battery of guns placed in position. The canals were filled in—no doubt that was necessary—and the area of the Water Gardens raised 5 ft. (by means of soil excavated when the London docks were made) and levelled to create the present grassy spaces of the South Grounds. An ordinary gravel path replaced Wren's splendid vista, and in the middle an obelisk was erected to the memory of soldiers who fell in the battle of Chillianwallah in 1849.

The trees of the Water Garden were uprooted, and the pollarded limes from the canal borders were removed to Lime Tree Avenue, an extension of the East Road. But very few of these trees remain; the planes that were planted in the Avenue seem to have had a deleterious effect on them. The Coal Creek was also filled in, and the wharf, water-stairs and little summer-houses removed or pulled down. *Sic transit gloria mundi!*

During Wren's time the inner quadrangles of Light Horse Court and Infirmary Court were open and gravelled, and later cobbled, to allow vehicles to enter and turn round comfortably; and in 1721 a well was dug in the centre of each. The beautiful ironwork well-heads which Wren designed were fashioned by the Hospital smith, William Winckles, and can still be seen. In 1817 the two courts were considerably altered by John Soane, Clerk of Works: the present lawns and shrubberies were planted and encircled by posts and chains. The roads flanking these courts were paved with unusually large cobblestones, some of which may be seen as the edging of a border just inside the gate of Ranelagh Gardens.

Inevitably one associates the Royal Hospital with Ranelagh Gardens which, from 1742 to 1803, were the favourite resort of the fashionable world. The Earl of Ranelagh was a clever and unscrupulous man who managed to acquire great riches during his term of office as Paymaster to the Forces in James II's reign. He obtained this land from the Hospital, built a house thereon, and laid out an elaborate garden. The property afterwards passed through several hands, and was finally leased to Lacey, the patentee of Drury Lane theatre, who turned it into a pleasure garden. It was a tremendous success. All the beaux and belles flocked there, and Horace Walpole wrote: "Every night constantly I go to Ranelagh, which has totally beat Vauxhall. Nobody goes anywhere else—everybody goes there. My Lord Chesterfield is so fond of it, that he says he has ordered all his letters to be directed thither."

A great Rotunda, nearly as big as the Albert Hall, was built in the grounds, with an arcade all round, and above it a gallery. The interior was decorated with paintings, mirrors, stucco, gilding and imitation marble, and there were forty-seven boxes, each furnished with a table and cloth, where the company could take tea and coffee. All kinds of entertainments were held—masquerades, illuminations and fireworks, public breakfasts, and evening concerts. For special occasions music was composed by Dr. Arne. And of course there was the never-failing diversion of walking about and looking at other people. As Bloomfield wrote in his *Wildflowers*, 1806:

> "We had seen every soul that was in it,
> Then we went round and saw them again."

No vestige of these splendours remains to-day. The Gardens afterwards reverted to the Royal Hospital, and were re-planned and re-planted very pleasantly between 1859 and 1866. With their beautiful trees, shady walks and undulating lawns they are now one of the most restful and secluded spots in which to spend a summer afternoon.

*　　　*　　　*　　　*

Some of these old London gardens are like pale wraiths of the past: nothing tangible is left of them. Some have so nearly vanished from our ken that they are only connected to the present day by one or two frail links that may snap at any moment. Some lie dreaming of bygone glory, wrapped in the peace of centuries. But some are still alive and vigorous to-day: with them the present has developed naturally out of the past like the growth of a tree. The roots are still there, and the plant is strong and vigorous and constantly putting forth fresh branches and foliage.

To this last class belongs the Chelsea Physic Garden. Ancient and modern exist side by side in this small and lovely plot of 3½ acres by the riverside; and to-day the Garden is doing more work than ever it did in the past. But before we embark on its romantic story it had better be explained that the Physic Garden is open to all students and teachers, but closed to the general public. With all its quiet beauty it is not a pleasure garden.

The work done there is threefold; purely botanical, teaching and research. The collection of plants and shrubs is based on their suitability for teaching botany as a pure science. Botanical specimens are supplied to all the Polytechnics, the L.C.C. schools in London and the Home Counties, to the hospitals such as Bart's and Guy's that are teaching medicine. London University alone has been supplied with 100,000 specimens.

The building along Royal Hospital Road includes a lecture hall and a working laboratory; and 4,000 to 5,000 students come here each year with their teachers to learn botany in the open. It must be delightful to study at the Physic Garden, for in long rectangular beds surrounded by grass and walks 100 Natural Orders are represented, and you can see the related plants growing side by side, instead of having to wait and hope, or hunt for a specimen, or having to be content with a mere picture of the plant. Students of advanced subjects such as biology also come with their teachers.

Then there is plant research. Colonial people, Indians and Chinese, sent by their Governments, are working here, and some are preparing for the English Doctorate of Science. But the work of the Garden is even more widespread than this. Seeds are exchanged with places all over the world—with Adelaide, New Zealand, France, Calcutta, the Crimea, South Africa, Helsinki, Leningrad, Moscow, Tashkent, Armenia, Tiflis, to quote a few at random.

And the headquarters of all this magnificent work is a small plot of land on the banks of the Thames. Though formally laid out, the Physic Garden looks far from formal, and presents an idyllic picture on a summer afternoon with its ancient trees that cast a welcome shade, its paths and sun-spattered lawns, long narrow beds and occasional little pools. At the central crossing of the walks stands the weather-worn marble statue of Sir Hans Sloane: it was carved by Rysbrach in 1733, and shows the great benefactor of the Gardens in his robes as President of the Royal Society. Not far from this figure stretches a long border of medicinal plants and old-time herbs that create a link between the past and the present.

What is the story behind this great achievement of the Physic Garden ? How did it come to pass ? To answer these questions we must go back to the seventeenth century. And the tale concerns every garden-lover, for we all, in one way or another, owe a debt to this institution.

Botanical gardens for the study of plants and herbs existed on the Continent long before this garden at Chelsea was founded in the reign of Charles II: there was one at Padua in 1545. The first in this country was established at Oxford in 1632, and later there was another at Westminster. It was not until 1673 that the Worshipful Company of Apothecaries (founded in James I's reign) obtained the lease of a garden 3½ acres in extent from Charles (afterwards Lord) Cheyne. The ground lay in the remote village of Chelsea, and the rent was £5 per annum for a term of 61 years. In those days botany and medicine went hand in hand, and the "Physicke Garden" was established for the study of medicinal herbs—though originally "physic" had not the narrow meaning of "medicinal," but was used in a broad sense for "natural" or "pertaining to nature."

Later the Company acquired the Westminster Physic Garden, and moved the plants that were there to Chelsea. By the time the lease of the Chelsea Gardens expired in 1722 Sir Hans Sloane was Lord of the Manor of Chelsea, and owned the property. He granted the land to the Apothecaries for ever for a yearly payment of £5, on condition that it should always be maintained as a Physic Garden. This arrangement lasted until 1899, when the Apothecaries gave it up, and the London Parochial Charities, supported by various smaller bodies, took it over.

Another condition imposed by Sir Hans Sloane was that the Company should every year give 50 new plants to the Royal Society (of which he was President) until 2,000 had been acquired. The Apothecaries, however, exceeded this number, for they continued the yearly gift till 1773, by which time they had presented 2,550 species of plants.

Before we go round the Garden let us note some of the people who helped to make it what it is to-day. Philip Miller was the first and perhaps most eminent curator. He was here from 1722 to 1771, and made the Chelsea Physic Garden the finest of its kind. He was the first botanist to realize the part played by insects in the fertilization of flowers; and to him we owe that famous work, *The Gardener's Dictionary*, for a long time the standard book on horticulture. During Miller's curatorship one incident at least had widespread repercussions. In 1732 he sent a small packet of cotton seed to Georgia, the new colony named after George II; and it is startling to reflect that from this insignificant little package three-quarters of the world's cotton has come!

After Miller a succession of well-known names were associated with the Garden. William Forsyth, whom we remember by the shrub forsythia, gave much attention to improving fruit trees; Sir Joseph Banks equipped and sailed with Captain Cook's expedition, named Botany Bay, and collected plants there; William Curtis, the author of *Flora Londoniensis* (1737), founded the *Botanical Magazine* in 1787; Dr. John Lindley was a copious writer on horticulture. The list goes on and on: there was Mrs. Elizabeth Blackwell, who wrote an eighteenth-century Herbal, and paid her father's debts by her exquisite drawings of medicinal plants; James Sherard and his brother William, founders of the Sherardian Professorship at Oxford University; Robert Fortune, the plant-hunter, who, disguised as a Chinaman, penetrated to remote parts of the Celestial Empire; Nathaniel Ward, inventor of portable "Wardian cases" for transporting plants; and many more.

Plant-collecting has always been an important branch of the Garden's work, and expeditions sent out during the eighteenth and nineteenth centuries have enriched our gardens considerably. Yellow jasmine, forsythia, weigelia, azaleas, magnolias, hydrangea, spiraea, camellias, plumbago and some chrysanthemums came to us at this time.

When the Apothecaries left Chelsea they took their library with them, but the Physic Garden is building up a good library of its own with many valuable and interesting books. Among the more personal documents is the diary of William Anderson, who was curator in 1815. This gives us glimpses behind the scenes. Labourers, we learn, were employed at a weekly wage of 18s. each—not a bad rate for those days. Dismissals are neatly noted on the yellowing paper, and reasons are given: "John Hutchins, discharged for a dunce," . . . "Henry Wood, too wise," . . . another man "for a blockhead." (Mr. Anderson sounds a little hard to please.) Other men were sent away for pilfering, for fighting, and for getting drunk on small beer.

Among the fine trees in the Garden the cedars were famous for two

THE ROYALL HOSPITAL AT CHELSEY

24   CHELSEA HOSPITAL: The garden lay-out in the early eighteenth century, with the L-shaped canals
From a plate in "Nouveau Théatre de la Grande Bretagne," IV, 1724

The Physick-Garden at Chelsea.

25 "The Physick Garden at Chelsea," in 1795.
From R. Phillips, "The Environs of London," II

centuries. They were amongst the earliest to be planted in England, and were brought over in 1684 as a gift from the Leyden Botanic Gardens. This was the first instance of a free exchange of plants between Botanical Gardens, and was the germ from which has sprung the world-wide exchange of to-day. The four cedars stood at the corners of a pond near the Embankment gate. Two had to be cut down in 1771, but two remained on either side of the gate, one till 1878, the other till 1904.

In place of this last pair of cedars two gingkos (*Gingko biloba*) have been planted, and no doubt will become equally celebrated—especially if they attain to their natural height of 130 ft.! A sacred Chinese tree, the gingko was until recent days supposed to have grown nowhere but in China, and also to be the only living tree surviving from the fossil age. But not long ago fossil specimens of the gingko were discovered in our own North country, thus proving that the tree grew in our forests before the Ice Age. Just imagine! It knew our prehistoric monsters, giant lizards and flying dragons. The Chinese found a resemblance to ducks' feet in the leaves of this tree, and so named it "gingko": we are reminded of the leaves of a certain delicate fern, and the gingko becomes the "maidenhair tree" for us.

And now another fossil tree has been discovered living in China. This is *Metasequoia glyptostroboides* (it has no popular name), which grows in a remarkable way developing a fresh "leader" each year while the former leader bends over to form a lateral branch. The Physic Garden possesses two small specimens of this tree, whose foliage changes to beautiful tints in the autumn.

Yet another Chinese tree, rare and ancient, is found here. Again there is no simple name for this glorious specimen of *Koelreutaria paniculata*, probably the first of its kind in England. It resembles a horse-chestnut slightly in that feathery spikes of tiny yellow flowers rise from whorls of dark pinnate leaves. The tinted fruits are large and bladder-like.

Other old trees are the pomegranate that is nailed against a wall, its scarlet flowers brilliant amidst dense glossy foliage; and the persimmon (*Dispyros Virginiana*) with an edible fruit the size of a black-currant, that does not become sweet and wholesome until it has been touched by frost. *Styrax officinalis* is used by makers of perfume: its leaves are bright green and shiny, and nearly as big as half-crowns. The tree yields a resin (*storax*) which has been used in the treatment of coughs since Roman times. As well as these treasures the Garden holds the largest yew in London, and a specimen of *Catalpa speciosa* that bears larger flowers than the kind one usually sees (*C. bignonioides*). The common catalpa was found near the Catawba river in Carolina by an expedition which Sir Hans Sloane sent out in the 1720's: hence the tree's name.

Olive, cork oak, locust acacia (*Gleditschia triacanthos*), holm oak, Caucasian beech (*Zelkova crenata*) and mulberry add to the great variety of trees to be seen in this comparatively small enclosure; and again we are struck by the number of trees, formerly considered exotic, that flourish in the smoky atmosphere of London.

Wandering along the gravelled paths of the Physic Garden, one's eye is caught by an unusual-looking rockery. It is the first recorded rock garden, and is made of rather extraordinary materials, i.e. 40 tons of *black* basaltic lava sent from Iceland by Sir Joseph Banks in 1772, and 50 tons of *white* stone from the Tower of London.

The tall iron gates leading to the Embankment were set up in 1877, and bear the crest of the Apothecaries. Through the narrow students' gate at the side in Swan Walk, with its caged bell and spiked bar above, we can see the barge-house where the Company kept their barge, a simple four-oared affair with a cabin amidships. But in those days, before the Embankment was built, the floor of the barge-house was 7 ft. lower than now: it stood actually at the river's edge instead of well inland.

The barge played a part in the "herborizing" expeditions which were a delightful feature during the Apothecaries' days. Five times a year their apprentices and other students used to meet very early in the morning and go botanizing with the Director. The outskirts of London were happy hunting grounds for these lads; the banks of the Thames by Wandsworth, Hammersmith and Putney were covered with wild flowers, and fritillaries grew in the Battersea fields. Sometimes the party went in the direction of Islington and Hampstead where, again, wild flowers abounded, and every year, in July, a longer trip was made to the sea or the mountains to collect specimens. The students would be away at least two days, and on their return would hold an exhibition of their finds, and invite distinguished guests to see it. There would be an address, and—the climax for some—a dinner given by the stewards of the Company.

Farther along the river bank, as we can see in old engravings, stood sheds for drying nets. Salmon-fishing was in 1787 an important industry of Chelsea. Since then the Embankment has changed the boundary of the Garden, enlarging it riverwards; and the line of the old river wall is indicated by square stones across the lower flower-beds.

The greenhouses help to show the scope of the work done here. There are eight of them, ranging in temperature from tropical to temperate, and they date from the taking over of the Garden from the Apothecaries: at the moment another is being erected for research work. The original heated houses were built for the reception of "tender greens," i.e. orange and lemon trees, and attracted a good deal of attention as they were among the earliest to be given a trial. Of course Evelyn came to see them, and on August 7th, 1685, he wrote:

"I went to see Mr. Watts, keeper of the Apothecaries' garden of simples at Chelsea, where there is a collection of innumerable rarities of that sort, particularly, besides many rare annuals, the tree bearing Jesuit's bark" (the cinchona, an early rarity, from which quinine is obtained) "which had done such wonders in quartan agues. What was very ingenious was the subterranean heate conveyed by a stove under the conservatory all vaulted with brick so as he has the doors and windows open in the hardest frosts, secluding only the snow."

That particular greenhouse no longer exists, but its tanks survive as fascinating little ponds in the flower-beds. One of the old unheated conservatories remains and holds a fine collection of ferns, including exquisite filmy ferns that are growing in an old Wardian case. During the last war the Gardens suffered from bombing, and the pot collection (plants in pots) was blown right out of the greenhouses. Many valuable plants were lost, but the survivors were gathered up, and Kew Gardens kindly gave them house-room.

Evelyn had already been to the Garden at an earlier date to see the new little cedars; and he must have been particularly interested in these 3 ft. shoots as it was he who introduced the cedar into this country. Tradition has it that Swift came here also. Pepys frequented the Swan tavern at the bottom of Swan Walk, but there is no evidence that he ever visited the Garden: it would lack the human society of which he was so fond. Nevertheless, before the Embankment was built, when the river washed the wall of the Garden, it must have been pleasant to sit under the trees and talk while the barges and boats slipped past on the tide (25).

In 1736 the great Swedish botanist, Linnaeus, came to the Garden and noted in his diary: "Miller of Chelsea permitted me to collect many plants in the Garden, and gave me several dried specimens collected in South America." Twelve years later, in 1748, another eminent Swedish botanist, Peter Kalm, was in England, and visited Chelsea. He, like Linnaeus, kept a diary, and in it described the Garden as "one of the largest collections of all rare and foreign plants, so that it is said in that respect to rival the Botanic Gardens of both Paris and Leyden."

Others have come here through the succeeding years—curators, professors and generations of students who were to be the botanists, apothecaries and doctors of medicine of the future. And still the endless procession goes on, and still in this lovely secluded spot important botanical work is carried out according to the conditions laid down by Sir Hans Sloane ". . . to the end that the said garden may at all times hereafter be continued as a Physicke Garden . . . for the manifestation of the power, wisdom and glory of God in the works of the creation."

CHAPTER X

More Famous Gardeners

Rose, London and Wise, Bridgeman, Kent, "Capability" Brown, Repton, Loddiges, Robinson

D URING the Commonwealth gardening styles remained fairly unchanged, but attention was given to orchards and what might be termed the useful side of horticulture. Then after the Restoration we find French ideas coming from the Continent with Charles II.

The best-known gardener of this period was John Rose, who was employed by the Earl of Essex at Cassiobury and at Essex House in the Strand. That nobleman sent him to Versailles to study under Le Nôtre. At this time France was to gardeners what Italy was to architects, the source of inspiration and new ideas. The gardens at Versailles were the wonder of the world, and Le Nôtre's ideas were being copied and adapted everywhere. Rose, after absorbing the new and grandiose French notions, brought them back to England and put them into practice, thus establishing what might be termed the Anglo-French school of gardening. He also learned much about the growing of "tender greens," which comprised orange and lemon trees and other delicate shrubs; and at Essex House the new-fashioned "cases" or conservatories for growing these "choice greens" soon became famous.

After the visit to France Rose was appointed Royal Gardener to Charles II. One of the gardening achievements for which he is remembered was growing the first pineapple in England; and a picture in Ham House shows him on bended knee presenting this unique fruit to the King. The background of the picture represents Dawney Park, Surrey, where pine-pits existed until fairly recent times. Pineapples were grown in all large gardens where there were hothouses, but the process of cultivation was long and costly. It usually took three years to obtain fruit: the first year of the plant's life was spent in the "propagation" or nursing pit, the next in the "successive" pit, and the last in the fruiting house, which had to be kept at a higher temperature. When easier communications with the West Indies were established it was found simpler and cheaper to import pineapples, and so the old pine-pits fell into disuse.

Like Sir William Temple, Rose was an authority on growing grapes, and in 1666 wrote *The English Vineyard Vindicated*.

One of his pupils succeeded him as Royal Gardener at the time of the revolution in 1688, and became very well known. This was George London, whose industry and talent his master soon recognized. After four or five years training Rose sent him to France for further improvement, and on his return London entered the service of Bishop Compton at Fulham Palace. In 1681 the young gardener became part-owner, with three others, of the famous Brompton Nurseries, close to Kensington; and when, by the death or retirement of the others, he was left sole proprietor, he took Henry Wise into partnership in 1694. This was the beginning of a long and fruitful association, for London and Wise supervised all the great gardens in England at this period.

London's royal appointment carried a salary of £200 per annum, and he was also made a Page of the Backstairs to Queen Mary. Soon after the Peace of Ryswick (1698) he accompanied the Earl of Portland, Ambassador Extraordinary to William III, into France, where he was specially interested in the fruit gardens at Versailles, and later wrote his *Observations* on them. He did much important work at Hampton Court, laying out the great parterre in box scroll-work that was so fashionable at the time. For this he had plenty of material to draw upon, for in *The Retir'd Gardener*, which London and Wise translated from the French of Louis Liger, no less than eleven sorts of parterres are described, with cut-work of grass, flower-beds and box-edgings that make patterns of scrolls or "embroidery like we have on our cloaths." (Those at Hampton Court were said to be like lace.) The paths or alleys between were filled with coloured sands, and a parterre was considered less troublesome to keep in order than a knot garden.

London supervised the removal of the large fountain at Hampton Court to the Chestnut Avenue in Bushey Park, and was responsible for that truly remarkable feat of digging up the 30-year old lime trees on the northern side of the semicircular avenue and replanting them south of the most southern row. The description and cost of this undertaking given in the accounts is staggering: "Four hundred and three large lime trees ye dimensions of them from 4 6^{in} to 3^{ft}, the charge of taking up these trees, bringing them to the place, digging holes of 10 or 12 feet diameter, carting 5 loades of earth to each tree one with another, with all charges 10s per tree, £201. 10."

The Brompton Nurseries were a flourishing concern and the largest of their kind in London. They covered more than 100 acres of ground, and contained an immense collection of plants. It was said that if each of these had been valued at only a penny the value of the stock would have exceeded £40,000. Queen Mary used to send her "tender greens" from Kensington Palace to be housed here every winter.

Of Henry Wise little is known personally save that he was born in 1653, and was also a pupil of Rose. He designed the grounds of Blenheim Palace, a job that took three years, and which was re-done in a later period. But his work with London will always be remembered. One of the partners' practical tasks in London was the effecting of a transformation at Kensington Gardens which William III began to lay out and Anne complete. This was turning an unsightly gravel pit into a sunken garden with a shrubbery of clipped trees and walks between.

Together, London and Wise translated *The Compleat Gardener*, a book on fruit and kitchen gardens by Jean de la Quintyne, who was Louis XIV's Director General of Fruit and Kitchen Gardens, and *The Solitary Gardener*, by Le Gentil, as well as *The Retir'd Gardener*, which dealt with more general aspects of horticulture. To all these works the partners added copious notes of their own, which makes it seem a pity that they did not write fresh books themselves instead of merely translating.

After the death of William III Wise was appointed to the care of the Royal Gardens by Queen Anne, and London then devoted his time to the famous gardens in various parts of England that were under the direction of himself and his partner. He visited them in turn, journeying on horseback and often covering fifty or sixty miles a day. It was this practice that finally brought about his death, for he caught a fever while travelling, and died after a fortnight's illness in 1717.

But before this he had the humiliation of seeing his elaborate scrollwork at Hampton Court uprooted by the Queen's orders. Was it because of her dislike for this parterre that she chose Wise to supersede London ? We are told that although she was living in the Palace as

Princess Anne at the time when the parterre was laid out the King did not consult her opinion on the matter. Possibly that slight rankled in the royal breast, possibly not. Or she may really have disliked the smell of box. We do not know.

As a garden-designer London was not particularly original, but he was skilful in adapting the large-scale French ideas to English surroundings. His knowledge of botany was not great, yet in the cultivation of fruit as well as of flowers he was unrivalled.

Wise remained in the royal service, and at Hampton Court, besides turfing the former parterre, he laid out the Broad Walk that runs past the eastern wing of the Palace. But it had no gorgeous herbaceous border; only on the opposite side were long, narrow box-edged beds containing clipped trees. He was reappointed head gardener by George I. The Brompton Nurseries were eventually made over to a gardener named Swinhoe; and Wise retired to Warwick and died there in 1738.

London and Wise were the last to design gardens entirely in a formal style. After their death a reaction against this fashion gradually set in, and this was not to be wondered at. In our ceaseless craving for change and so-called improvement each generation despises the work of the preceding age, and thinks it has better ideas. Formal gardens, Tudor, Italian, French and Dutch, had been popular for so long that a change was bound to come. But it did not happen suddenly. We get the first hint in the Dutch *clairvoyées* or grilles which afforded "vistas" or views beyond the garden, thus apparently extending its boundaries. Bridgeman, a successor to London and Wise as Superintendent of the Royal Gardens, went a step further: he kept the old walks with high, clipped hedges, but did away with confining walls, thereby making the garden one with the surrounding park or country. And to help this effect of unity he used the sunken fosse between garden and country, which came as such a surprise to people wandering through the garden that they exclaimed involuntarily, "Ha-ha!"—thus giving the ditch its name which has lasted until now.

William Kent (1684–1748) did away with formality. He "leaped the fence and saw all Nature as a garden"—and so the English school of landscape gardening was born. To copy Nature was its aim; and winding paths and streams, knolls crowned by clumps of trees, gentle undulations of land, avenues and long perspectives of trees were enthusiastically introduced into the great gardens. And flowers were banished. They had no place in these noble landscapes, but lurked in kitchen gardens and small enclosures, awaiting the time when they would once more be appreciated.

Kent himself (27) was that rare phenomenon, an all-round artist— painter, decorator and designer of furniture, sculptor, architect and landscape gardener, and, what is more, practising these various branches of art simultaneously. Because of this versatility he has been misjudged and condemned. In an age given over to specialization a " Jack-of-all-trades" is automatically considered "master of none," and so it has been with William Kent. But he was actually a survival of the Renaissance tradition wherein an artist developed his ability in many branches of his art. Kent was a poor painter, a mediocre sculptor, and his architecture was unoriginal; but his interior decoration was superb, and so was his furniture. Incidentally, he was the first English architect to design furniture. For his garden architecture we have to rely chiefly on what was written and said, as the most important of the gardens he designed no longer exist; but they are what made his great reputation.

He claimed to be the inventor of the more natural style of gardening, which was afterwards developed by "Capability" Brown and others: and his chief aim was to create a suitable setting for the classical buildings of the time. Although he completely ignored or forgot the fact that these Italianate mansions would, in their country of origin, be surrounded with terraces, colonnades, fountains, topiary work and extremely formal gardens, he was successful in making a most appropriate and English background for his buildings. As far as London is concerned, the avenues and Gardens at Kensington are his work, as well as the decoration of some of the rooms in the Palace; and he also designed the grounds of Chiswick House for his patron, the third Earl of Burlington.

Kent's rise to fame was spectacular. Born in the North Riding of Yorkshire, and first apprenticed to a coach-builder, this prodigy came to London at the age of nineteen to study painting, and was sent to Rome by friends. In Italy he met the Earl of Burlington, who interested himself in the youth, brought him back to England, and gave him rooms in Burlington House for the rest of his life. With the gift of charming manners and an air of authority Kent soon became popular in high society, and was consulted on all matters of taste. He went to

Rome again in 1719 and in 1730 to study architecture and buy pictures for Lord Burlington. His very first commission was to decorate the Cupola Room at Kensington Palace for George I, in place of Thornhill, the foremost painter of the time, and thereafter his name was made.

Horace Walpole said of him that "he was painter enough to taste the charms of landscape, bold and opinionated enough to dare to dictate, and born with a genius to strike out a great system from the twilight of imperfect essays." And here is an impression of his work:

"The pencil of his imagination bestowed all the arts of landscape on the scenes he handled. The great principles on which he worked were perspective and light and shade. Groups of trees broke too uniform and too extensive a lawn. . . . The gentle stream was taught to serpentine at its leisure; and where discontinued by different levels, its course appeared to be concealed by thickets, properly interspersed, and glittered again at a distance, where it might be supposed naturally to arrive. Its borders were smoother but preserved their waving irregularity. A few trees scattered here and there on its edges, sprinkled the tame bank that accompanied its meanders, and when it disappeared among the hills, shades descending from the heights leaned towards its progress, and framed the distant point of light under which it was lost."

What Kent began Lancelot Brown continued (26). This eminent landscape gardener gained his nickname of "Capability" from the fact that whenever he was consulted about laying out a garden he would express the opinion that it "had capabilities." He was born in Northumberland in 1715, and began his career as a kitchen gardener, at first to a gentleman in Woodstock, and then to Lord Cobham at Stowe. In 1750, through the influence of that nobleman, he became head gardener to the Duke of Grafton at Wakefield Lodge, where his planning and execution of the lake brought him into prominence. He was next appointed Royal Gardener at Hampton Court and Windsor. Fortunately for us, he refused to make any alterations in the grounds at Hampton Court; but we can be grateful to him for planting the celebrated vine. His next post was at Blenheim, where he created the fine artificial lake in a week. That feat established his reputation. Thereafter he became the fashion, and all the nobility and gentry who wanted to lay out new gardens or alter old ones flocked to consult him.

The passion for imitating Nature now over-reached itself. From one end of England to the other the axe rang and the spade was wielded, and so rapidly was the face of the country being altered that in 1772 Sir

William Chambers declared that if the mania was not checked, "in a few years more 3 trees would not be found in a strait line from the Land's End to the Tweed."

It was impossible for Brown personally to keep pace with the commissions that poured in upon him. He employed assistants, and developed a kind of formula for his designs, irrespective of whether or not it suited the garden under consideration: he could never have invented sufficient new plans for all the gardens he was asked to design. And so his style gradually degenerated into a mannerism. He was unrivalled in his treatment of water, but his gentle slopes, plantations and clumps of trees seldom varied; and this monotony, added to the weak work of his imitators, eventually hastened the decay of landscape gardening.

The question has often been raised as to whether Brown was a genius or a charlatan. Good taste he certainly had, but he never attained to the heights of invention and achievement reached by his predecessor, Kent; and he swept away much beauty in the course of his "improvements." Lovely old gardens were ruthlessly sacrificed, century-old avenues destroyed, terraces levelled. . . . It never seemed to occur to these ruthless gardeners, Brown and his followers, that an ancient avenue or yew hedge was beautiful in itself.

> "Improvement too, the idol of the age,
> Is fed with many a victim. Lo, he comes!
> The omnipotent magician, Brown, appears!
> Down falls the venerable pile, the abode
> Of our forefathers. . . .
> He speaks—The lake in front becomes a lawn;
> Woods vanish, hills subside, and valleys rise,
> And streams, as if created for his use,
> Pursue the track of his directing wand."
>
> (Cowper: *The Gardener*)

The "omnipotent magician" made a great fortune out of landscape gardening and architecture, and rose to the dignity of High Sheriff of Huntingdonshire in 1770. Thirteen years later he died.

By the end of the eighteenth century landscape gardening was recognized as the natural gardening style of England; and just as we had formerly copied gardening ideas from the French and Italian, so now they imitated us. But when Humphry Repton (1752–1818) appeared on the scene people were beginning to realize the mistakes Brown had made, and to regret his wholesale destruction of ancient gardens and historical relics. Repton admired the work of his predecessors, and described his own as "landscape gardening," using the term for the first time; but he was influenced by those who criticized, and consequently was less drastic in his "improvements." He was more anxious to gratify the pre-conceived wishes of his patrons than to strike out on an original line of his own. Notes and plans of individual gardens as they appeared before and after alteration were collected by him and bound in red morocco, and each owner received the "Red Book" of his own garden.

Although he wrote many books on the subject, Repton did not confine himself to landscape style, but adopted more natural and varied ideas. Bog-gardens, rock gardens, lawns, and the training of climbing plants on poles or hoops were advocated by him. Best of all, he began to bring flowers back, and made provision for flower gardens "detached and distinct from the general scenery of the place." In London he altered Kensington Gardens, and laid out Russell Square, the next largest square to Lincoln's Inn Fields. In his book on Landscape Gardening Repton explains at length his reasons for the design of Russell Square in 1810, and expresses the hope that:

"A few years hence, when the present patches of shrubs shall have become thickets—when the present meagre rows of trees shall have become an umbrageous avenue—and the children now in their nurses' arms shall have become the parents or grandsires of future generations—this square may serve to record that the Art of Landscape Gardening in the beginning of the nineteenth century was not directed by whim or caprice, but founded on a due consideration of utility as well as beauty, without a bigoted adherence to forms and lines, whether straight, or crooked, or serpentine."

Visitors to Russell Square can judge for themselves whether this hope has been fulfilled.

Several more names stand out in London gardening during the eighteenth century. There were the men connected with the Chelsea Physic Garden, whom we have already met; and J. C. Loudon (1783–1845), landscape gardener, Fellow of the Linnaean Society and writer on horticultural subjects. He founded *The Gardener's Magazine*, and ran other monthly periodicals. There were many well-known nursery gardens flourishing at this period: Fairchild was at Hoxton, James Lee

26 LANCELOT ("CAPABILITY")
    BROWN (1715–1783)
*From a portrait by Nathaniel
            Dance*

27 WILLIAM KENT (1684–
              1748)
*From a portrait by Bartholomew
            Dandridge*

28 HAM HOUSE, Surrey, 1780
From the painting by Thomas Rowlandson

at Hammersmith, James Gordon (who introduced the gingko) at Mile End, Green at Brentford, and others at Putney, Fulham, Lambeth, Battersea and Hyde Park Corner. Incidentally, it was Thomas Fairchild who left money for the annual Fairchild Lecture to be delivered annually on Whit-Tuesday in St. Leonard's, Shoreditch, the subject to be either "The Wonderful Works of God in Creation," or "On the Certainty of the Resurrection of the Dead, proved by the certain changes of the animal and vegetable parts of the Creation."

But the largest and most famous nursery garden was that of the Loddiges at Hackney. A contemporary writer describes it admiringly: "Such a collection of plants as is in the possession of Messrs. Loddige, does not exist elsewhere in the world. The stock if sold at the retail prices is worth £200,000. . . . Altogether there are in their Gardens and Houses 8,000 species exclusive of 2,000 varieties." And when we read further that besides being well known as orchid growers they had 1,393 species and varieties of roses, the fame of this nursery is justified. Loddiges' name is associated with his *Botanical Cabinet*, the most celebrated illustrated book on flowering plants, which he compiled between 1818 and 1833. It was issued in twenty volumes and had 2,000 hand-coloured plates.

The earlier Loddiges, Conrad, has another claim to our remembrance, for he introduced the common, mauve rhododendron (*R. ponticum*), a native of Asia Minor, the southern Caucasus and Southern Spain, into this country. Soon after 1756 he "sold the first plant to the Marquis of Rockingham, a noble encourager of botany and gardening." The new shrub took so kindly to English soil, and flourished so prolifically, that now it is one of the most popular evergreens and can almost be reckoned as one of our "wild" flowers.

Botanical and horticultural research were carried out eagerly in the early years of the nineteenth century: the Chelsea Physic Garden and Kew Gardens were active in this respect, and expeditions were sent out to remote spots of the earth. The advent of so many new flowers from foreign countries gave rise to the practice of "bedding-out," in which the chief object to be attained was vivid colour. Geraniums, calceolarias, lobelias and salvias were crammed into flower-beds, and made a brilliant and even startling show from Midsummer to Michaelmas, but left a dreary blank for the rest of the year after they were removed.

This state of affairs was finally remedied by William Robinson

(1838–1935). "Carpet-bedding" was anathema to him, for he believed in simplicity and the natural beauty of plant growth as opposed to these artificial arrangements. He developed a new style known as "wild gardening," and brought back hardy plants and more permanent flowers to provide a succession of interest. Three centuries before, Francis Bacon's ideal had been to have flowers blooming in the garden during every month of the year, and at last—very long last—gardeners began to realize that this object was attainable. Robinson believed in masses of colour, in grouping and contrasting flowers, in naturalizing plants in shrubberies, on grassy banks and in wild places; in fact, he was the founder of the flower-garden as we know it to-day. He may be said to have invented the herbaceous border, and he was one of the pioneers of the rock-garden. Another of his innovations was the planting of plane trees in London, and we owe the welcome shade of these trees along the Victoria Embankment to his suggestion. The wonderful herbaceous border which he laid out at Hampton Court is his abiding memorial in flowers; and his books, *The Wild Garden* (1881) and *The English Flower Garden* (1883), keep alive his ideas.

29 Vignette from Humphry Repton's *Fragments on the Theory and Practice of Landscape Gardening, 1816*

CHAPTER XI

Private Gardens

Ham House—Chiswick House

BOTH these gardens are now thrown open to the public, but because they were designed originally as private gardens they figure here as such.

The history of Ham House began in 1610 when it was built as a country residence by Sir Thomas Vavasour, Knight Marshal to James I. An expression of his loyalty can be seen to-day in the wish VIVAT REX carved on the north door with his initials and the date of building. Half-way through the century the property was bequeathed to Elizabeth, Countess of Dysart, by her father. In 1672 she married as her second husband the Earl (later to be Duke) of Lauderdale, a man whose ambition and thirst for power nearly equalled her own; and the house and its furnishings still bear the impress of her violent, ruthless personality. The Duke became a member of the notorious "Cabal" ministry of Charles II, and one of the rooms at Ham House (the Queen's Bedchamber) is known as "The Cabal Room." But it is extremely doubtful that the council ever met there: the building and decorating of the room was not completed until after the Ministry was dissolved.

The Lauderdales lived extravagantly, decorating the house sumptuously, and filling it with luxurious furniture and appointments and rather mediocre pictures, so that it soon became necessary to enlarge their home. This work was carried out from 1673 to 1675, and the original "H" shape of the building had the space between the wings on the south side enclosed, thereby adding a new series of apartments facing south on to the long terrace.

With the house and its treasures we are not here concerned, but the gardens make a fascinating study: they have passed through so many phases. First, we have a contemporary plan of the house and garden (reproduced in the guide-book) which was made between 1610 and 1615 by John Smithson, the Jacobean architect. This shows a long rectangular "inner courte" before the north entrance, with "the Principall garden," 240 ft. square, on the east of this court, and corresponding on the other side a "Backe Courte" of the same area. On the south front of the house stretched "gardens and orchards," 436 ft. by 300 ft., and this space was planned to contain a fairly elaborate parterre having formal flower-beds set with trees at regular intervals, and gravel walks and grass between.

Whether this was ever laid out as designed we do not know: nothing remains for our guidance. But when Evelyn visited the mansion in 1678, he wrote in his diary:

"After dinner I walked to Ham to see the House and Garden of the Duke of Lauderdale, which is indeed inferior to few of the best Villas in Italy itself; the House furnished like a great Prince's; the Parterres, Flower Gardens, Orangeries, Groves, Avenues, Courts, Statues, Perspectives, Fountains, Aviaries, and all this at the banks of the Sweetest River in the World, must needs be admired."

Of all this magnificence only the Orangery remains, and this is now a tea-house. It is a pretty building of old red brick, with tall windows from floor to ceiling; and the wistaria that clothes it, and the lavender beneath the windows evoke a wistful remembrance of the past. Opposite, on the other side of the wide lawn, is a short avenue of ancient holm oaks with a weather-worn stone Bacchus in the middle. This may be one of the avenues that Evelyn admired.

Another interesting feature, outside the Orangery, is a rather rare "Tree of Cavalry" (*Palyurus spina-Christi*), from one of which the Crown of Thorns was believed to have been made. The branches are pliable and exceedingly spiny, and the fruits which follow the delicate spikes of minute yellow flowers are flat and disk-like, resembling nothing so much as tiny low-crowned, broad-brimmed hats of greenish yellow. With its low and widespreading growth, this is a picturesque tree.

Between 1670 and 1683 outdoor interests at Ham strayed indoors, for the strong-minded Duchess, now widowed, converted one of the bed-chambers into an aviary and called it the "Volary Room." Here she collected and kept "outlandish birds"—a fashion of the day, and we only wish that some record of these could be found to tell us what birds she had: it might be possible to link them up with those that Charles II was keeping in St. James's Park and Birdcage Walk at this time. The name of the "Volary Room" still persists, but not the purpose for which it was set aside. The King visited Ham House on several occasions, and we may be sure that he and the Duchess discussed their "outlandish birds." It is said that the iron entrance gates, which date from the time of James I, have never been opened since the last departure of the second Charles. In the house, above one of the chimney-pieces, can be seen a copy of the picture that shows John Rose presenting the first pineapple grown in England to the Merry Monarch.

One of the alterations which the Lauderdales made to the house in 1679 was inserting niches and busts above the ground-floor windows on the north side and in the curving walls of the forecourt. Originally of lead or marble, these heads have been replaced by stone busts. The river-god in the centre of the forecourt belongs to a later date, the end of the eighteenth century. It is made of artificial "Coade" stone, a material much used in that period for modelling architectural features.

Two fine avenues lead up to the house, and legend has it that Hood composed his poem, "The Elm Tree," while strolling here. We get a glimpse of the grounds as they were in 1770 from a letter written by Horace Walpole: his niece had married the fifth Earl of Dysart, who had a great dislike of visitors:

"I went yesterday to see my niece in her new principality of Ham. It delighted me and made me peevish. Close to the Thames, in the centre of all rich and verdant beauty, it is so blocked up and barricaded with walls, vast trees and gates, that you think yourself an hundred miles off and an hundred years back . . . because the gates never were opened by his (Lord Dysart's) father but once for the late Lord Granville, you are locked out and locked in, and after journeying all round the house as you do round an old French fortified town, you are at last admitted through the stable-yard to creep along a dark passage by the housekeeper's room, and so by a back-door into the great hall. He seems as much afraid of water as a cat, for though you might enjoy the Thames from every window of three sides of the house, you may tumble into it before you would guess it was there."

It is pleasant to turn from this gloomy picture to a painting by Rowlandson, dated 1780, in the time of the same Earl and Countess (28). In the background we see the south face of the house with its long terrace, and a central flight of steps descending to the lawns which are divided by walks. The Earl and Countess are advancing from the end of the broad central walk to a lovely garden that makes the foreground of the picture. He wears the Order of the Garter, she, on his arm, has her train borne by a page; and a bowing figure is welcoming them to some kind of *fête champêtre*. The garden which they are entering has a series of formal, clipped hedges curving away like parallel screens on either hand. Then the greensward opens out towards the spectator in a great semicircle of slim, feathery trees, beneath which are ranged statues on pedestals. Gaily dressed figures in perukes and long brocaded coats, fichus and rich overskirts are strolling or talking together beneath the trees, dogs are gambolling, and there is an air of festivity about the scene. It is charming in its Watteau-like freshness and delicacy.

This lay-out, too, of the garden has disappeared, leaving us with only a painted vision of the past. And there seem to be no further records or descriptions.

After being in the possession of the original Countess of Dysart's descendants, the Tollemache family, for more than 300 years, Ham House and its gardens were generously presented to the National Trust in 1948 by Sir Lyonel Tollemache, Bart., and Mr. Cecil Tollemache. The arrangement of the house and its contents is in the hands of the Victoria and Albert Museum; and the Ministry of Works is responsible for the gardens.

During the war these naturally had to be neglected, and when gardeners once more came to work they found a tangled and impenetrable wilderness comparable only to that which surrounded the castle of the Sleeping Beauty. But a transformation was speedily effected, and now the great unbroken stretches of lawn and their bordering woods make a beautiful and dignified setting for the house. Hidden in the woods are ancient trees of box, old acacias, fine Spanish chestnuts and holm oaks of a bygone time. The long gravelled terrace is in summer ablaze with flowers, and on the walls of the house one discovers immense magnolias (*M. grandiflora*), lemon verbena and wistaria. Ham House is still a place of enchantment with its restful expanses of greensward and brilliant flowers, its long red brick walls and old paved courtyards, its graceful iron gates and the forecourt with busts leaning eagerly out from their niches.

The gardens are still in process of being re-arranged, and it will be interesting to see what is done here. Is it too much to hope that by degrees part of the grounds, at any rate, may be reconstructed in Restoration style to match the house in expressing that period?

*   *   *   *

The famous garden of Chiswick House is a palimpsest upon which it is still possible to trace a succession of designs like partly erased drawings; and as we wander about the 66 acres of grounds we can discover odd forgotten or overlaid bits, and fit them into their proper places. Save for the avenues in Kensington Gardens, this is the only garden design by William Kent remaining in or near London, and it is exceptionally interesting as combining Italian and English styles.

Yet we cannot regard it to-day as a full and true picture of Kent's work: he himself might not recognize it. A garden is not a static thing —it grows and changes every year, and a mere decade is sufficient to alter its aspect. For instance, when Kent planted the Lebanon cedars in the avenues 200 years ago they were small and shapely shrubs spaced out between the statues which dominated them. Did he plant them to be effective at the time or in ten or twenty years' time? It is hardly likely that he planned for centuries ahead. However that may be, the balance of his design is now reversed: the statues have shrunk to stone pygmies beneath the massive, spreading boughs of the cedars.

And so it is with other trees and with the vistas that Kent planted: the trees have grown or been cut down or replaced with different species, the vistas are overgrown or blocked up. But in spite of this the framework, or what might be called the "bones" of his garden, remains —the statues and urns and obelisks (30, 31), the temple and the lake, the bridge, the winding paths in the wilderness. And the spirit of his work lives on, for in whatever direction one looks, from whatever point in the garden, a picture meets the eye.

Following the curve of a path, one comes suddenly upon a quiet green hollow that holds a circular pool with an obelisk in the centre. From this rise grassy terraces dotted with young cypresses like green candle-flames; and brooding over the hollow is a little domed temple with a portico, set among trees and shrubs. . . . The 2,000-ft. long lake breaks into view with swimming mallards disturbing the reflections of trees;

and the long stretch of water leads the eye inevitably to the elegant, balustraded bridge at one end. . . . Along a vista cut through woodland, the grass lies like patches of emerald velvet; through the leaves on either side sunshine filters down on to the grey boles of beeches and the brown trunks of cedars, and dapples a slim chestnut veiled from top to bottom in green. At the end of the shady vista, in full sunlight, stands a tall, dazzling white obelisk. . . . Nearer the house the foliage of trees makes a veritable symphony in green: the strong, blackish green of cedars is seen against silver-green, pure green, grey-green, yellowish green, green in all its shades. . . .

These are some of the pictures one can see in the garden.

The house is a fit centre of all this loveliness, and now that the side wings (designed and built by James Wyatt in 1788) have been demolished, this little gem of architecture is restored to its pristine state, with its portico and graceful double staircase on the north side, and a cupola setting a crown on all.

This is not the first building on the site: it was preceded by a Jacobean mansion that had a chequered history and passed through many hands. But we know that the garden was productive, for in 1631, when the Earl of Somerset was banished to Chiswick House with his wife for their supposed share in the murder of Sir Thomas Overbury, his Lordship tried to curry favour again with James I by sending gifts of fruit—"peaches conceivably good, and all that was left of the plums"—from the garden. Further, the Earl promised that if the King would give him a good gardener there would be an annual present of garden produce. His Majesty, however, was not beguiled by these suggestions.

To-day a tall gate of ironwork between ball-topped piers leads into the great kitchen garden where presumably this fruit was grown. It is still bounded by walls of incomparable red brick, and at the far end a vine-hung doorway leads into another equally large walled garden, turfed and holding an aged medlar and a short avenue of fruit trees.

About 1682 Chiswick House was bought by the first Earl of Burlington; and much later, in 1716, Richard Boyle, the third Earl, returning from his travels in Italy with an accumulation of pictures, statuary and other works of art, decided to build a villa on this site to accommodate his treasures. This house is not, as has been often stated, a reproduction of Palladio's Villa Rotunda near Vicenza, but is merely derived from

30 The Temple terraces as originally set with potted orange trees and an obelisk and sunken pool

31 The Canal and Temple

Both from paintings by Pieter Rysbrack
THE GARDENS OF CHISWICK HOUSE BEFORE 1736

32   The Cascade, and a part of the Canal

33   The approach to the front of the House

Both from Carrington Bowles' prints
CHISWICK HOUSE ABOUT 1750

the Palladian style which his lordship admired so much. It was never intended to be a dwelling-house, but was planned as a museum—a fact which made pointless the sneer of Lord Hervey, Vice-Chamberlain to George II, that "the Earl of Burlington had built a house too small to live in, and too great to hang on one's watch-chain," referring to the fashionable large fob and seals worn by beaux of that period. The interior decoration is by Kent, and the arrangement of rooms communicating with each other is admirable for displaying works of art and for social receptions.

The brilliance of these entertainments can be gauged from the fact that Lord Burlington was a generous patron of art and letters and music. Kent, as we already know, was a permanent member of his household. Gay lived with him for some time, Pope was an intimate, coming and going as he pleased. Swift had the *entrée* of his house, and Handel was his guest for some time. These friends of his must often have been at Chiswick; and with such lavish expenditure in one direction and another it is not surprising to find that the Earl died impoverished. But before that happened David Garrick and his wife·spent their honeymoon at the villa.

The gardens at Chiswick House were developed before the villa was built between 1730 and 1732. Bridgeman is said to have begun them before Kent returned from Italy in 1719, and this may partly account for the formal lay-out near the house; but Kent succeeded him, and the "architect Earl" and his *protégé* must have worked together in great enjoyment, one designing the house, the other planning the grounds (32, 33). The appearance of the garden in its early days can be seen in Kent's drawings and also in Rocque's engravings (1736); and Phené Spiers, in *Memorials of Old Middlesex*, has given us this word-picture of the grounds near the house; it is interesting to compare it with what survive to-day:

"Long vistas in front of the principal rooms of the villa are laid out in greensward flanked by avenues of cedar or lime trees, gravel paths between hedges of clipped yew, and in the former case terminated with semicircular alcoves in cut myrtle; containing niches filled with statues or vases. . . . In front of the villa was a great avenue 400 ft. long, with a double row of cedars and lime-trees, terminated by a semicircular exedra formed of cut myrtle, in the niches of which were placed vases and antique statues, 3 of which (brought from Hadrian's villa at Tivoli) are still *in situ*."

The cut hedges have disappeared, the three Tivoli statues have been removed to another part of the gardens; otherwise the original plan remains.

Traces of tall clipped hedges occur in many places. Mingling with other trees in the Wilderness, one comes across spectral yews, 19 or 20 ft. high, gaunt and sparsely foliaged; and careful observation will discern that they must have formed the walls of alleys now overgrown or completely lost (34). And also in the Wilderness is more of Kent's work. Believing that one essential of a picturesque garden was inequality of the ground, he not only created terraces and slopes and hollows, but made sunken walks; and some of these can be found serpentining between banks of earth. They not only give a sense of seclusion, but by their deviousness add to the distance to be traversed, thus increasing the apparent area of the ground. This was a favourite device of the landscape gardeners, and was probably evolved in the first place from the maze or labyrinth.

The semicircular Italian garden is laid out in formal flower-beds and graced by stone urns and terminal busts set against a background of trees. To one side lies a pebbled pavement of geometrical design that is the floor of the former orangery. The conservatory which stretches across the whole width of this garden contains magnificent camellia *trees* that grow to the roof—the Chiswick camellias are famous. And the wistaria that wreathes the building along its whole length should be noticed. A fine gingko tree is probably as old as the house; and other contemporary trees, besides the cedars, are a huge hybrid oak (*Quercus suber*) and a tulip tree (*Liriodendron tulipfera*).

After the death of the Earl of Burlington Chiswick House passed to his daughter, whose husband became the fourth Duke of Devonshire, and successive generations of this family lived here until well into the nineteenth century. The sixth Duke was a keen horticulturist, and did much to improve and develop the gardens. He commissioned Paxton to build a conservatory which was later succeeded by the present one. A lady friend of Horace Walpole wrote in 1813:

"Drove with the Duke of Devonshire in his curricle to Chiswick, where he showed me all the alterations that he was about to make, in adding the garden of Lady Mary Coke's house to his own. The house is down, and in the garden he has constructed a magnificent hot-house, with a conservatory for flowers, the middle under a cupola; altogether it is three hundred feet long. The communication between the two gardens is through the old greenhouse, of which they have made a double arcade, making the prettiest effect imaginable."

This Duke brought to Chiswick the magnificent gates of gilded wrought-iron that until the end of the last century stood at the Duke's Avenue entrance. They belonged in the first instance to Lord Heathfield, and adorned his grounds at Turnham Green: when Heathfield House was demolished in 1837 the Duke bought the gates. In 1897 they were removed from Chiswick to Devonshire House, Piccadilly, and finally in 1921 were bought by the nation out of the balance of the Queen Victoria Memorial Fund, and erected on the Piccadilly border of the Green Park, where they now remain, looking somewhat isolated.

But if Chiswick House has lost one gate it still retains another of great historic interest. At the end of the broad gravel walk along the north side is the Inigo Jones gateway. Originally this stood in the garden of Beaufort House, Chelsea, which had been Sir Thomas More's home, and in 1736 was bought by Sir Hans Sloane, who demolished it. But he was aware of Lord Burlington's admiration for the work of this architect, and presented the gateway to the Earl. The stone tablet on the left bears the inscription, "Builded by Inigo Jones at Chelsea MDCXXI," and on the right, "Given by Sir Hans Sloan, Baronet, to the Earl of Burlington MDCCXXXVIII."

Not only was the sixth Duke of Devonshire interested in horticulture; he had a great love of natural history, and kept at Chiswick a menagerie that included elks, emus, "and other pretty sportive death-dealers," kangaroos, an Indian bull and cow, "goats of all colours and dimensions," and even an elephant in an enclosure near the house. When Sir Walter Scott visited Chiswick in 1828 he wrote in his diary for May 17th:

"A numerous and gay party were assembled to walk and enjoy the beauty of that Palladian House. The place and highly ornamental garden belonging to it, resembles a picture by Watteau. There is some affectation in the picture, but in the *ensemble* the original looked very well. The Duke of Devonshire received me with the best possible manners. The scene was dignified by the presence of an immense elephant, who, under the charge of a groom, wandered up and down, giving an air of Asiatic pageantry to the entertainment. I was never more sensible of the dignity which largeness of size, and freedom of movement give to this otherwise very ugly animal."

To Chiswick House in 1806 came Charles James Fox, the great Whig statesman, in search of health. At first the beauty of the garden seemed to revive him, but within a fortnight he was dead. The same thing happened with George Canning, who died here in 1827.

In later years King Edward VII had the house for a time; and "The Princes' Gardens" is the spot where his children tended their own little flower-beds. Then the villa was leased to Dr. Tuke, who used it for a mental asylum till 1929; and in 1948 the house was taken over by the National Trust. The garden, or rather, park, as it is termed to-day, is the responsibility of the Brentford and Chiswick Urban District Council.

CHAPTER XII

Royal Gardens

Buckingham Palace—Kensington Palace

IN spite of all his faults James I cared for his kingdom, and often tried to do what he thought good for it. But he was an unpractical idealist and his enthusiasm was not backed by the knowledge and concentration necessary to carry his schemes to a successful issue; consequently many of them came to nought.

Among his well-intentioned failures must be reckoned the project to establish a silk industry in England by means of silkworms. In his letter to the Lord-Lieutenants of the counties, introducing the idea in 1609, we read what was in the King's mind:

". . . having sene in a few yeares space past, that our brother, the French king, hath, since his coming to that crowne, both begunne and brought to perfection the making of silks in his country . . . whereby he hath wonne to himself honour, and to his subjectes a mervailous increase of wealth, would account it no little happiness to us, if the same worke . . . might, in our time, produce the fruits which it hath done."

There we have the vision in a nutshell. What France had accomplished England could achieve: the King would gain prestige and honour, his subjects would become rich. And it was all so easy. One bought silkworms, one planted mulberry trees for their food, and the obliging larvae did the rest. The scheme went ahead. A pamphlet on the cultivation of mulberry trees, the breeding of silkworms and the making of silk was published; the Lord-Lieutenants were ordered to announce that in the following March a thousand mulberry trees would be delivered to each county town, and all people who could were required to buy them at the rate of 6s. per hundred or 3d. each. Up and down the country, in gardens large and small and in open spaces, mulberry trees

were planted; and it is quite likely that some of the more aged specimens we see to-day are survivals from that general planting.

In London four acres of waste land outside the western boundary of
St. James's Park—and therefore fairly near the royal Palace of Westminster—were enclosed for his Majesty's use as a silk farm. This plot
was known as the Mulberry Garden. Walls were built round it, the
ground was prepared, hundreds of mulberry trees were planted—and
then expenses for the Garden began to accumulate at an alarming rate.
There were no profits—for a very simple reason. The King was not a
botanist, and in his enthusiasm failed to realize that there are two
species of mulberry trees—the white, which is suitable for silkworms'
food and little else, and the black which produces the delicious edible
berry but does not tempt the caterpillar. James had ordered black
mulberry trees instead of white! And so while people picked heavy
crops of mulberries for market the silkworms died of starvation.

Year after year the Mulberry Garden was a heavy charge on the royal
purse until some time between 1628 and 1654, when it was closed down
as a commercial proposition, and Goring House was built on part of
the site for the Earl of Norwich.

But the Garden reappears as a public pleasure resort in Evelyn's
diary for May 10th, 1654:

"My Lady Gerrard treated us at Mulberry Garden, now the only place of
refreshment about the town for persons of the best quality to be exceedingly
cheated at; Cromwell and his partisans having shut up and seized on Spring
Garden which till now had been the usual rendezvous for the ladies and
gallants of this season."

The Garden became immensely popular, especially after it was
patronized by Charles II and his Court. An atmosphere of romance
hung over the place. Beneath the leafy mulberry trees and along the
shady paths lovers might linger; the silkworms' houses were converted
into restaurants where excellent food and wine were served; and arbours
cunningly hidden about the grounds invited dalliance. Pepys found the
Garden silly and dull on his first visit, but later changed his opinion.
One day he spent 18s. there on refreshment for his friends, and in
April, 1669, enjoyed the food, and was "mighty merry" with a company of gentlemen.

Popularity, however, does not last, and this phase, too, of the Mulberry Gardens came to an end. It was finally closed in 1673, and the property was granted by Charles II to Henry Bennet, Earl of Arlington, who enlarged the grounds by acquiring more land. In 1674 Goring House was burned down, but was rebuilt as Arlington House and furnished most extravagantly. After the Earl's death it passed to his daughter, the Duchess of Grafton, who let it to the Duke of Devonshire.

Stow described the house as "a most neat Box, and sweetly sealed amongst gardens, beside the prospect of the Park, and the adjoining fields"; and from another writer we get a brief account of the garden:

"Arlington Garden . . . is a fair place, with good walks, both airy and shady. There are six of the greatest earthen pots that are anywhere else, being at least ten feet over within the edge, but they stand abroad, and have nothing in them but the tree holy-oke, "(hollyhock ?)" an indifferent plant, which grows well enough in the ground. Their greenhouse is very well, and their green-yard excels, but their greens are not so bright and clean as farther off in the country, as if they suffered something from the smutty air of the town."

The property was next sold to the Duke of Buckingham, and in 1703 we find him erecting another house close to the site of the old one, which he demolished (35). The new mansion was considered the most beautiful in London. It was a red-brick building with a square centre, and was topped by a balustraded parapet and leaden statues. On either side were wings, attached by a colonnade to the main part of the house: in front lay a great railed courtyard with a fountain playing in a stone basin. This, with other fountains, was supplied from a leaden cistern above the rooms in one of the wings. The tank, which held 50 tons of water, was filled from the Thames by means of an engine.

The gardens must have been charming. Henry Wise was in charge, and he planted avenues of lime trees and laid out formal grounds. From the Surveyor General's report in 1698 we learn that these included "the Oval Court and Flower Garden, the Terrace Walk, the Dwarf Tree Garden, the Wilderness, the Grove and Bowling Green, the very extensive Orange Houses with the Bagnio, Bathing Cisterns and the like."

But the best description is given by the owner himself in a lengthy letter to the Duke of Shrewsbury in 1709, telling him how he spent his time after resigning the post of Privy Seal to Queen Anne. He describes the house in great detail, and then continues:

"To these gardens we go down from the house by seven steps, into a gravel walk that reaches across the whole garden, with a covered arbour at each end of it. Another of 30 ft. broad leads from the front of the house, and lies between two groves of tall lime trees planted in several equal ranks upon a carpet of grass; the outsides of these groves are bordered with tubs of Bays and Orange trees.

"At the end of this broad walk, you go up to a Terrace 400 paces long, with a large Semicircle in the middle, from whence is beheld the Queen's two parks, and a great part of Surrey; then going down a few steps you walk on the banks of a canal 600 yards long, and 17 broad, with two rows of Limes on either side.

"On one side of this Terrace a Wall covered with Roses and Jassemines is made low to admit the view of a meadow full of cattle just under it, (no disagreeable object in the midst of a great City) and at each end a descent into parterres with fountains and water-works.

"From the biggest of these parterres we pass into a little square garden that has a fountain in the middle, and two greenhouses on the sides, with a convenient bathing apartment in one of them, and near another part of it lies a flower garden. Below all this, a kitchen-garden full of the best sorts of fruit, has several walks in it fit for the coldest weather.

"Only one thing I forgot, though of more satisfaction to me than all the rest, which I fancy you guess already, and 'tis a little closet of Books at the end of that greenhouse which joins the best apartment. . . . Under the windows of this closet and greenhouse, is a little wilderness full of black birds and nightingales. . . ."

This then was the appearance of Buckingham House and its garden when George III bought it in 1761 as a place to which he and Queen Charlotte might retire when they wished for a more homely and domestic existence than the Court of St. James afforded. Later it became a dower-house for Charlotte instead of Somerset House, the former residence of the Dowager Queens, and was known as Queen's House.

By that time the gardens were considered old-fashioned: formality was out-of-date, and George IV, as well as having the house rebuilt by Nash, had the garden transformed. Under the cloak of "repairs and improvements" Queen's House was pulled down and a new building, popularly known as Pimlico Palace, and also as St. George's Palace or New Palace, rose in its place. The work was begun in 1825 under the

34 CHISWICK HOUSE about 1750: "A View of the three Walks terminated by the Cassina, the Pavilion, and the Rustic House," seen from the back of the house

From a Carrington Bowles' print

35   GORING or ARLINGTON HOUSE (1632), later Buckingham House
From a water-colour in the British Museum

36   BUCKINGHAM PALACE. The Nash façade (1825) from St. James's Park
The Marble Arch stands in its original position
From a print of 1843

supervision of Nash, and was not completed till 1835, when William IV was on the throne. The grounds were re-planned from designs by Nash which were carried out by William Aiton the younger, son of the royal gardener at Kew and Kensington, who wrote *Hortus Kewensis*. Most of the lime trees were cut down, fountains and canal, terraces and parterres were done away with, and five acres of ornamental water, with bays and a promontory and a few clumps of trees, took their place. The whole effect was starkly bare and conventional at first, but later the hard outline of the lake was broken by trees, and the promontory was converted into an island (36).

When, at the beginning of her reign, Queen Victoria decided to make Buckingham Palace her official residence, she called in Edward Blore, who had been special architect to her uncle, William IV, to make alterations in the building and the grounds. He made a fish-pond and laid out parterres and shrubberies; and with the earth that had been removed to make the lake he raised a large artificial mound and planted it with shrubs and trees to hide the view of the stables from the Palace windows. Then in 1843 Blore transformed a conservatory at the southwest corner of the building into a private chapel.

In 1844 a pavilion was erected in the garden and decorated with frescoes by Landseer, Maclise, Eastlake and other contemporary artists. This summer-house is referred to in the diary of Mr. Uwins, one of the artists employed, when he describes the daily life of Queen Victoria and the Prince Consort:

"In many things they are an example to the age. They have breakfasted, heard morning prayers with the household in the private chapel, and are out some distance from the Palace, talking to us in the summer-house before half-past nine o'clock, sometimes earlier. After the public duties of the day, before their dinner, they come out again, evidently delighted to get away from the bustle of the world to enjoy each other's society in the solitude of the garden. . . . Here, too, the Royal children are brought out by their nurses, and the whole arrangement seems like real domestic pleasure."

This summer-house was renovated during Edward VII's reign, but it no longer exists. A pretty little garden house was, however, brought from the old Admiralty Gardens at the beginning of the century. The roof is supported by carved wooden figures, and it is possible that the whole thing was designed by William Kent about 1730. Near it stands the colossal Waterloo Vase, carved from a single block of marble, which was made as a memento of the battle of Waterloo.

The present park-like arrangement of the 40-acre garden remains pretty much as it was in Queen Victoria's day, with splendid trees, a lovely lake, and magnificent lawns that in their smooth green texture rank among the finest in the country.

*   *   *   *

It will be remembered that Hampton Court was chosen by William III for a residence chiefly because the air suited him. But that Palace was a long way from London, and meant constant journeying to and fro as well as delay in transacting important State business; and so the King searched for somewhere to live that would be nearer Whitehall and yet away from the smoky air of the city on account of his poor health. Eventually he found just what he wanted in the rural mansion of Nottingham House at Kensington, and purchased it in 1690.

This was a fairly new house. Only in 1662 had Charles II given certain parts of Hyde Park, at the Kensington end, to Secretary Heneage Finch who later became Earl of Nottingham and Lord Chancellor. This nobleman built a small country mansion on his new estate, and called it Nottingham House; and it was his son who sold it to King William. But as it stood it was far too small for a royal residence. The King therefore commissioned Sir Christopher Wren to build a new upper storey and south wing, and at once began to lay out the 26 acres of grounds afresh.

Soon after these alterations were begun Evelyn came to see the property, and wrote in his diary in 1690: "I went to Kensington which King William had bought of Lord Nottingham and alter'd, but 'twas yet a patched building, but with the garden however it is a very sweete villa, having to it the Park, and a straight new way through the Park." By the next year further progress had been made, for Gibson described the gardens as

"not great nor abounding with fine plants. The orange lemon and myrtles with other trees they had there in summer, were all removed to Mr. London and Mr. Wise's greenhouse at Brompton Park, a little mile from there. But the walks and grass laid very fine, and they were digging up a flat of 4 or 5 acres to enlarge their garden."

It has now been established that Le Nôtre did not actually come to work in England in spite of entreaties from Charles II; but he may have designed the new gardens at Kensington for William III, and as London, the King's gardener, had visited France to see the remarkable garden schemes of Le Nôtre, French influence, as well as Dutch, was marked throughout the gardens.

Work went on apace during William's reign. London and Wise supervised the levelling and turfing of lawns, the making of paths, planting of trees, and all the details of construction. Queen Mary, bustling about Hampton Court and personally overseeing the alteration of the gardens there, found time to attend to Kensington as well. Switzer (who was a pupil of London and Wise) tells us that "This active Princess lost no time but was either measuring, directing or ordering her Buildings, but in Gardening, especially Exoticks, she was particularly skilled and allowed Dr. Pluknet £200 per ann. for his Assistance therein."

In 1691 part of the "new house" was burnt down, but the damage was soon repaired, and the grounds were unaffected. Then in 1694 Queen Mary died, and after this sad event the King took no further interest in the gardens. Evelyn described them at this date as "very delicious," and so they remained until William's death.

Queen Anne spent a good deal of time at Kensington Palace, and effected many improvements in the gardens. One of the first, planned and carried out by London and Wise, was the transformation of a gravel pit which marred the approach to the Palace from Kensington. This was converted into a sunken garden embellished with hedges of yew and variegated holly clipped in the form of bastions, fortifications, scarps and counterscarps, and was known as the "siege of Troy." It was a truly formidable example of topiary work, and in 1711 or 1712 Addison wrote in No. 477 of *The Spectator*: "It must have been a fine genius for gardening, that could have hit the eye with so uncommon and agreeable a scene as that which it is now wrought into."

Switzer also had something to say about this feat: "The place where that beautiful Hollow now is, was a large irregular Gravel-pit, which, according to several Designs given in, was to have been filled, but that Mr. Wise prevailed, and has given it that surprizing Model it now appears in. As great a Piece of Work as that whole Ground is, 'twas near all completed in one Season, (viz.) between Michaelmas and Lady

Day, which demonstrates to what a pitch Gard'ning is arrived within these twenty or thirty years." What a pity this garden has not survived for our present-day approval or otherwise! Its site, to the north of the Palace, is now built over, and no one could guess at what lay there before.

More land was now acquired for the royal gardens, and Wise was put in charge of them (42). To quote a contemporary writer: "Her Majesty has been pleased lately to plant near 30 acres more to the north, separated from the rest only by a stately greenhouse, not yet finished." This was of course Wren's beautiful Orangery, which some say was used in the first place as a banqueting-house, and also for entertainments and fêtes. It was converted or re-converted into a conservatory or orangery after the Court finally left in 1760.

Box edging was removed from the flower-beds at Kensington as well as at Hampton Court. Switzer praises Queen Anne for "Rooting up the *Box*, and giving an *English* model to the old-made Gardens at Kensington." He must have been referring to the "Flower-Ground" shown in Rocque's plan of 1736. It lay to the north of the Palace, and had probably been laid out in the Dutch style by King William. This garden, too, has disappeared.

George II (or, rather, his indefatigable Queen, Caroline) had the splendours of Versailles in mind, and took 300 acres from Hyde Park to add to the Palace gardens. Now something on a really large scale could be designed, and Bridgeman was set to work. He planned the three great avenues radiating from the Round Pond, which are reminiscent of Le Nôtre's style. They were planted about 1727, and must be far lovelier now with the trees in full maturity than when they were first set out. The vistas are completed with works of a later date. G. F. Watts' equestrian statue of "Physical Energy" makes a superb climax to the central avenue, and the Speke obelisk is satisfying at the end of the north-eastern vista.

Bridgeman was also responsible for the Round Pond, or "The Bason," as it was originally called; and probably the two Broad Walks. He made a sunken "ha-ha" to form a boundary between Kensington Gardens and Hyde Park; and with the earth thus removed created a mount and set a summer-house on top. This stood near the western end of Rotten Row, and after it was levelled the gate there was still for a long time known as the Mount Gate.

Here is the impression that these improvements made upon a contemporary writer, Bickham:

". . . the gardens of Kensington Palace, which are 3½ miles in circumference, are very fine; and have been much improved and enlarged since his present Majesty came to the throne, under the care and management of the late ingenious Mr. Bridgeman. They are kept in the greatest order; and in summer time when the court is not there, are resorted to by a vast concourse of the most polite company."

After Bridgeman came Kent, who continued the planting of the avenues. Most of this work remains, and as one walks through the Gardens, appreciating the main avenues where many of the original stately elms are still standing, the shifting perspective of trees continually resolves itself into other subsidiary avenues in a pleasant and surprising manner. It was here that Kent carried his passion for imitating Nature to such a pitch that he even planted dead trees in the grounds!

Queen Caroline, in her enthusiasm for gardening, converted the dozen or so marshy ponds in Hyde Park into a "Serpentine River," as we know it to-day. She would have liked to close St. James's Park and turn it into a private garden for the palace of that name; but when she approached Sir Robert Walpole and asked him what the cost would be, he replied drily, "Only three crowns," and the Queen was wise enough to desist.

Few changes were made in Kensington Gardens between this time and 1840. Repton did a little work; and then the Court ceased to reside at the Palace, and the grounds were thrown open to the public during the summer. This residence is, of course, closely associated with Queen Victoria: as a child she walked or drove in a little carriage in the grounds nearly every day. At this Palace she began her reign and held her first Court; but as Queen she lived at Buckingham Palace. She did not, however, forget the home of her childhood, and we owe her the great privilege of visiting these gardens as well as those of Hampton Court and Kew. In 1839 Kensington Gardens were declared "open all the year round, to all respectably dressed persons from sunrise to sunset."

About 1840 the drainage of the Gardens was improved, turf was re-laid, old high walls not already taken down by Bridgeman were demolished and iron railings set up in their place, new trees and shrubs were planted. When the Albert Memorial was erected opposite the great rotunda of the Hall, an alteration was made in some of the avenues of the Gardens, and a fresh avenue of planes and elms was planted, leading straight to the Memorial. This, one of the most criticized monuments in London, was designed by Sir Gilbert Scott as a mediaeval reliquary or shrine on a large scale. Bearing that in mind makes it easier to accept and appreciate the style of architecture and the elaborate detail to which so many people object. Behind the Memorial runs the Flower Walk that with its long succession of beds is a joy throughout the summer months.

Early in this century the beautiful sunken garden was made. It resembles, but is not an exact copy of, the pond garden at Hampton Court. Oblong in shape, it is surrounded by a low brick wall with piers and iron gates in the middle of each side. Shallow, turfed terraces with beds of brilliant flowers descend to a stone pavement that surrounds the long narrow pool. In the water rise three antique cisterns of lead, from which little fountains play; and round the pool are set square stone boxes filled with more flowers. Round three sides of the garden runs a leafy tunnel of pleached limes with "windows" or peep-holes left in the foliage; and through these one may view the lovely sunlit garden and its flowers. On the fourth side is a screen of limes, also with peep-holes.

A small part of the old gardens close to the Palace on the south and east has been retained and kept private for the residents; and on the east side a statue of Queen Victoria, erected by her daughter, Princess Louise, looks across the Round Pond to Hyde Park. There is one other statue that is peculiarly appropriate to the Gardens where countless children have played and sailed their boats for more than a hundred years. This is the figure of Peter Pan, the boy who remains the symbol of eternal childhood.

Kensington Gardens are indeed the children's playground. On any fine day you will see perambulators with Nannies seated beside them, knitting and keeping a watchful eye on toddlers stumbling along the paths. Older children will be playing games under the trees, their high, shrill voices and laughter mingling with the joyous barking of dogs who are scampering after sticks thrown for them. The blue water of the Round Pond and the scudding sails repeat the blue sky and white clouds overhead. And in the background the old red Palace, comfortably ensconced among its trees, looks out benevolently upon the scene—the same scene year after year, but with different little actors.

CHAPTER XIII

Further Royal Gardens

The Royal Botanical Gardens, Kew

JUST as the gardens of Hampton Court are strongly reminiscent of the Tudors, so Kew is full of Hanoverian associations, and even to-day the Gardens wear a royal air. In the past kings and queens, princes and princesses have lived here and have left their imprint on the grounds; and the spacious lawns and vistas, glades of magnificent forest trees, lakes and formal gardens, conservatories and brilliant masses of flowers have a grandeur that lifts them to royal rank. No recent upstart planting is here, but the slow growth of centuries that has matured to rich perfection. And when to this is added the scientific work that makes Kew the centre of botanical science in the British Commonwealth, it will be realized that the Gardens are unique.

Kew goes back a long, long time in history. The village was mentioned in Domesday Book, and its name has been spelt variously as Kaye, Keye, Kahoo and Kayhough. Possibly there was a quay for barges here. Snugly situated beside the river and away from the streams of traffic, the village was able to preserve its rural atmosphere longer than many other suburbs of London. Nothing of importance ever happened there: it owes its fame purely to royal associations and the royal gardens.

The piece of land between Kew Bridge and Richmond Bridge was originally several properties, the most important of which were the demesne of Richmond Lodge and Kew House. Richmond Lodge (also known as Ormonde Lodge) was not the old historic Richmond Palace, but a private residence which did not come into royal hands until about 1721, in the reign of George II. To the previous house on that site Cardinal Wolsey had retired in 1530 after his fall from power; and after his death royal servants and private gentlemen lived there till 1707, when Queen Anne leased it to the Duke of Ormonde. He demolished the old house and built another on the site. When he was impeached in 1715 his estates were forfeited; but six years afterwards the Richmond property was restored to his brother, the Earl of Arran, who disposed of it to the Prince of Wales, later George II.

Richmond Lodge became a favourite retreat of the King and Queen; and here, as at Hampton Court and Kensington, the indefatigable Queen Caroline plunged into gardening with, first, Bridgeman and then Kent as her advisers. Bridgeman is said to have introduced "cultivated fields and even morsels of a forest appearance" into the royal gardens at Richmond; and in his time or Kent's parts of the garden were wild (and even now are spoken of as "the Wilderness"), parts were wooded and intersected by winding paths (as at Chiswick House) and separated by cornfields and meadows. Near the house the garden was more formal (again like Chiswick), and a great part of the present Deer Park was crossed by avenues of trees.

Roughly, the gardens formed a narrow triangle with the apex near the present Kew Palace, the base consisting of Richmond Green and part of the Old Deer Park, with the Thames forming the western side, and Love Lane the eastern. This lane, or rather, bridle-path, ran from south to north, practically bisecting the present Gardens and following the present Holly Walk and Stafford Walk pretty closely.

The Queen endeavoured to give interest to the gardens by erecting fanciful buildings haphazardly. One of the most extraordinary (and said to have been designed by Kent) was Merlin's Cave, which stood to the south-west of the present lake. It was a kind of wood-and-plaster summer-house with three circular rooms, the central one higher than the others. Topped with conical thatched roofs they resembled nothing so much as tall bee-hives, and contained waxen effigies of a most incongruous company, Queen Elizabeth and Merlin among them. There were also scattered about the grounds a curious Hermitage north-east of the lake, a temple, a dairy-house which was used for its proper purpose, and the Queen's Pavilion.

So much for Richmond Lodge. Kew House, the first of the three "palaces" of Kew, belonged in the seventeenth century to the Bennett family, and later passed to the Capels through the marriage of a Bennett daughter with Sir Henry (afterwards Lord) Capel. Sir Henry was a keen gardener, and to him we owe the beginning of a horticultural centre at Kew. John Evelyn frequently came to see his garden, and com-

40 The Hermitage
41 The Chinese Temple

39 The Chinese Pagoda

From engravings after H. West, 1832
KEW GARDENS

37 The Temple of Victory
38 The Ruined Arch

175

42 KENSINGTON PALACE: The formal la~
From a plate in "Nouveau T

the Gardens in the early eighteenth century
la Grand Bretagne," IV, 1724

43 KEW GARDENS: The artificially-ruined Triumphal Arch, built by Sir William Chambers in 1759-60

From the painting by Richard Wilson, 1761-2

mented on it at various dates. According to him it had "the choicest fruit of any in England," and its owner was "the most industrious and understanding in it." Evelyn refers to two greenhouses there for oranges and myrtles; and on February 24th, 1688, writes: "We went to Kew to visit Sir Henry Capel's, whose orangery and myrtetum are most beautiful and perfectly well kept. He was contriving very high palisades of reeds, to shade his oranges during the summer, and painting those reeds with oil."

John Gibson, in his *Short Account of Several Gardens near London*, 1691, remarks that Sir Henry "has four white striped hollies about four feet above their cases, kept round and regular, which cost him five pounds a tree this last year; and six laurustinuses he has, with large round equal heads, which are very flowery, and make a fine show. . . . His flowers and fruits are of the very best."

Lord Capel had no children, and Kew House was inherited by his grand-niece, Lady Elizabeth Capel. Her husband, Mr. Samuel Molyneux, was interested in astronomy, and turned part of Kew House into an observatory, and built a telescope. And there, in 1725, Dr. Bradley (later Astronomer Royal) discovered the aberration of light and the nutation of the earth's axis. The sundial on the lawn in front of the present Kew Palace commemorates these discoveries and marks the site of the old house where they were made. When Lady Elizabeth died in 1730 the Kew property was leased by the Capel family to Frederick, Prince of Wales; and thus began the long and close association of Royalty with Kew Gardens, which only came to an end in 1904 with the death of the Duke of Cambridge who lived in Cambridge Cottage, now Museum IV.

This house held many memories for Queen Mary. The Duke was her grandfather, and as a child she used to play in the garden under the old chestnut on the lawn and among the lilacs and lilies.

Frederick made many alterations in the grounds with the help of Kent, and did some additional planting. After his death in 1751 his widow, Princess Augusta of Saxe-Gotha and mother of George III, took over the responsibility of the gardens; and it was she who began the laying-out of a Botanic Garden at Kew in 1760, which was to prove the embryo of the present immense and important scientific establishment.

The area selected for the Botanic Garden was about nine acres; it lay just inside what is now the main entrance, and was enclosed by walls. In the middle of the plot stood the Temple of the Sun; and one part of the ground was called the Physic Garden, and was given up to herbaceous plants arranged according to the "new" Linnaean system. Another part, the Arboretum, was devoted to trees and shrubs similarly classified; and the remainder of this garden was known as the Pleasure Ground.

In 1760 was built the "Great Stove" or hothouse—the largest in England at that time, being 114 ft. long. Down the middle lay a "bark stove" or bed of tan 60 ft. long, which gave off heat by fermentation, and into which pots of plants were thrust. To-day the wistaria which once grew on the walls of the "Stove" is trained on a circular iron cage, thus marking the site of the hothouse.

The Dowager Princess appointed John Stuart, third Earl of Bute, as scientific director; William Aiton, who had worked at the Chelsea Physic Garden under Miller, as head gardener; and Sir William Chambers as architect. Sir William was also the designer of Somerset House, and in the course of his travels had learned a good deal about foreign architecture, especially Chinese. Consequently we find him erecting at Kew such exotic structures as the Mosque, the Alhambra and the Pagoda as well as a ruined arch and temples which were a conventional feature of every gentleman's garden in the eighteenth century (37, 38, 39, 40, 41).

The Mosque and the Alhambra no longer exist; the 163-ft. high Pagoda might be described as the "signature" of Kew. It has ten stories that gradually diminish in diameter, and when first built must have been a resplendent sight, for each roof-angle bore a carved Chinese dragon decorated with coloured glass that glittered in the sunshine. The shining white Temple of the Sun was destroyed in 1916 by a gale which sent a great Lebanon cedar crashing on to it. The site is now marked by a young gingko tree planted by Queen Mary on November 27th, 1923, and an inscription.

Loveliest of all Sir William's garden buildings is the little circular, domed Temple of Aeolus (rebuilt in 1845) which on its wooded knoll provides a perfect background for drifts of daffodils in springtime. The small Temples of Bellona and Arethusa, the Orangery (now Museum III) and the ruined arch leading to it (43) are the only other surviving structures of those that were then dotted about the Gardens.

The Japanese gateway near the Pagoda belongs to a much later date. It was presented by Japanese exhibitors after the White City Exhibition in 1910, and is a replica of the famous "Chokushi-Mon" at Kyoto.

In 1772 Princess Augusta died, and the control of Kew passed to her son, George III, who moved his residence from Richmond Lodge to Kew House, and united the two properties by purchasing the freehold of Kew House from the Essex family. "Farmer" George inherited his love of the soil and fondness for gardening from his mother. He lived happily and simply with Queen Charlotte at Kew House, often dining on mutton and boiled turnips. And for her he built the Queen's Cottage among the woods in what used to be the royal garden of Richmond Lodge. This picturesque but uncomfortable little dwelling was not planned to be lived in, but just for picnics. It is divided into two parts, each containing one room upstairs and one down, and to get to the kitchens without going outside you must go up one flight of stairs and down another. Here the Queen used to dispense tea on summer afternoons while the royal children played about in what is now the bluebell wood and bird sanctuary—a quiet and lovely spot for royal ghosts to wander in.

The Rhododendron Dell (also in the Richmond Lodge garden) was designed by "Capability" Brown, who was now head gardener, and many buildings that were considered unsightly were pulled down— Merlin's Cave, the peculiar Hermitage and some of the temples among them. Perhaps the most beautiful achievement of this period was the laying out of the Syon vista, that fine avenue of holm oaks leading across the grass from the Palm House to the river's edge and framing a view of Syon House, crowned by its lion, on the opposite bank of the Thames. During the late eighteenth century the Syon vista was a fashionable promenade on Sunday evenings, and the fine lords and ladies of London used to saunter up and down and quiz each other. And sometimes the King used to arrive on the scene in a royal boat shaped like an enormous swan.

By this time Kew had become one of the most important scientific institutions in the world; and on the death of Lord Bute the King appointed Sir Joseph Banks, the great scientist, to be the unpaid Director of the Gardens. Under his *régime* plant collectors were sent out to distant parts of the world—Asia, South Africa, the Americas, Australia and China—to search for and bring home exotic plants; and this was the main activity of Kew to the end of the century. It must have been an exciting time for those who waited at the Gardens; they never knew what strange seeds, plants, shrubs or trees might arrive next. The first collector, Christopher Smith, sent home pelargoniums and cinerarias; and after that bread-fruit, the monkey-puzzle tree (*Auracaria imbricata*), Cape heaths, tree-peonies, New Zealand flax, varieties of fuchsia and hydrangea were some of the newcomers.

Both George III, and Sir Joseph Banks died in 1820. The King had been insane for some years and unable to appreciate the increasing beauty of Kew, though his clouded mind seems to have retained a sense of gardening. Queen Charlotte's death had taken place two years before the King's, and previously there had been changes. Kew House had been demolished in 1802, and the "Dutch House" (built in 1631 by Samuel Fortrey) had become the Palace: this was closed after the Queen's death, and Kew ceased to be a residence of the ruling sovereign.

Thereafter the Gardens began to decline in repute and usefulness. Neither George IV nor William IV was interested in gardening, and early in Victoria's reign there was serious thought of doing away with the Botanic Garden; the cost of upkeep was a heavy drain on the Privy Purse, and the young Queen had no personal associations with Kew. However, public opinion was so strongly against abolishing the Gardens that in 1840 they were made over to the nation by Queen Victoria, and placed in charge of the Commissioner of Woods and Forests, then transferred to the Office of Works. Since 1903 the Gardens have been controlled by the Ministry of Agriculture and Fisheries. At the time when it became national property Kew included not only the Botanic Garden, 15 acres in extent, but also the Pleasure Grounds, a kitchen garden, fruit and forcing houses, a melon yard, greenhouses and pits.

Under its new Director, Sir William Hooker, who was appointed in 1841, Kew entered upon another period of great progress. The grounds were thrown open to the public, another 45 acres were added; and in 1845 it was decided to transform the Pleasure Grounds into an Arboretum, thus increasing the area of the Gardens to 250 acres. (To-day they comprise 300 acres.) Other additions during the nineteenth century were the Palm House, designed by Decimus Burton and for a long time the largest plant house in existence; the improvement of the pond near it; the founding of the Museum of Economic Botany, the Herbarium and botanical Library. Burton was also responsible for the imposing gates at the main entrance, and the Temperate House which holds plants from South Africa, Australia, the temperate regions of the Himalayas and Chile. (A new conservatory is now being built close by for the housing of Australian plants.)

The lake—an entirely artificial creation—was excavated, and a new orchid house built to take the fine collection from Woburn presented by the Duke of Bedford. The main walks were laid out by W. A. Nesfield, and so were the formal gardens, but these were simplified in 1881. The sending out of plant collectors was resumed, and Kew became a national institution with connections all over the world.

Sir William died in 1865, and was succeeded by his son, Sir Joseph Hooker, and then by Sir William Thiselton-Dyer and other gifted men who carried out further improvements. But such a wide and firm foundation had been laid by Sir William Hooker that successive directors had only to build upon it. During the latter half of the nineteenth century the picture gallery containing the paintings of Miss Marianne North was opened. This intrepid woman at the age of forty began to travel in search of subjects for her brush. Between 1872 and 1885 she visited fifteen countries, and after that six more, braving danger in jungles, swamps and rivers. The result was a marvellous collection of water-colours depicting flowers, trees, birds and butterflies, many of them unknown in Europe at that time. These 800 studies she presented to Kew together with the gallery to contain them. The Jodrell Laboratory, which does important work connected with physiological botany, was established about the same time.

Statistics have a fascination for some people, who, if they go to Kew, can find much to nourish their passion for figures. Botanical specimens amount to 45,000 varieties, including 10,000 trees and shrubs; and many thousands of different flowers are annually raised from seed. The Herbarium holds six million botanical specimens, and the Library 45,000 books on botanical subjects. Every year the Director deals with about 10,000 postal enquiries; and about 8,000 packages of seeds and plants are sent out. Visitors to the Gardens number one and a half million annually; and it must be borne in mind that *all these figures are steadily increasing.*

A romantic story could be written about Kew's share in the encouragement of industries in the British Commonwealth by the distribution of

seeds and plants. For instance, cinchona, the quinine tree, was introduced from South America via Kew to India, thus saving millions of
lives. Rubber seeds were sent home by collectors, and thousands of
plants were raised from them at Kew. These were then despatched to
Malaya and Ceylon, and multiplied into great rubber plantations.
Coffee, bread-fruit, pineapples and bananas; paper materials, fibres,
vegetable oils, timber and medicinal plants have been similarly
distributed to new centres—and the work goes on.

From the landscape point of view the Gardens were further developed
by avenues planted in the Arboretum. New plant-houses were erected
and more entrances made. The rock-garden was begun in 1882,
primarily to hold a bequest of more than 2,000 Alpine plants; and here
we can see plants from nearly all the chief mountain ranges of the
world flowering happily on the outskirts of London! The bamboo
garden, the sunk rose-garden and the lily pond came into being, still
further additions were made. . . .

And so by degrees Kew became the paradise we know and love.

Wherein lies its spell ? It is not primarily a pleasure garden but a great
scientific centre, a botanical adviser to all Government departments, a
kind of university for advanced students of botany; and it contains the
richest plant collection in the world. These things do not necessarily
make for beauty: how is it that Kew is so entirely satisfying in the
aesthetic sense?

Surely its charm lies in the way it is laid out. Under wise directorship
Kew has grown to be a perfect example of English landscape gardening,
with trees, lawns, water and flowers used in broad and dignified
effects. Think of the avenues that have been planned—the Syon vista,
the Pagoda vista, the Thorn Avenue where crataegus and pyrus mingle
so delightfully, the Holly Walk and the Woodland Walk, to mention
just a few. Recollect the magnificent expanses of turf that form such an
effective foreground for the trees—and the lake, after the lapse of
years, appearing as a lovely "natural" feature that mirrors the sky.
Willows and water-lilies add to its attraction, as do waterfowl of many
kinds. The formal pond near the Palm House is in character with the
garden there; and the water-lily pond has transformed an old gravel
pit.

Then there are the gardens, formal with flower-beds near the Palm
House, prodigal with roses or lilies, stiff with gloriously coloured

blooms in the iris garden. The informal gardens might be termed "flower meadows," so exquisite is the scatter of crocuses, gold, white and purple in the grass under bare trees, so breath-taking the thousands of daffodils nodding in the wind. In the wild garden below the Temple of Aeolus one also finds in due season tiny pink cyclamen, blue anemones, meadow saffron and Christmas roses. And who can ever forget the bridal beauty of cherry blossom near the Palm House, and the glory of bluebells massed in the woods near the Queen's Cottage, with the fugitive sunlight deepening their cobalt to rich purple that fades again to misty grey?

Many types of visitors go to Kew. There are gardeners, both professional and amateur, who seek to enlarge their knowledge of plants, to learn names, find out what is most suitable for their own gardens, and discover the latest additions. There are students of botany to whom Kew opens her treasures, not only out of doors but in the numerous glasshouses, four museums, the Herbarium, Library, Jodrell Laboratory and the North Gallery of pictures. There are artists and photographers who seek for beauty here and find it. And then—the great majority— there are the people who come simply because Kew is a lovely garden. They crowd in through the gates, knowing little or nothing about flowers or trees, botany or gardening; but they can rest or wander about happily in the fresh air, admiring this and that, absorbing beauty (perhaps unconsciously), and perhaps only half-aware of the rapturous bird-song around and above them.

Kew is one vast sanctuary for birds: the shyest lose their timidity and flutter at one's feet. No less than eighty kinds are found there, and the air is vibrant with their music. Every imaginable sound of whistling, fluting, twittering and warbling goes on all day long through the spring and summer. One can spend hours trying to identify unfamiliar calls that come from the woods, the tree-tops and distant bushes. And even in autumn and winter there is bird-song.

At whatever season one goes to Kew there is something lovely to be seen. There are always flowers in the hothouses, and out of doors the long procession of the year begins to unwind itself with snowdrops and crocuses, and continues with daffodils and magnolias, flowering crabs and cherries, azaleas, bluebells, lilac, irises, rhododendrons and roses and a wealth of flowers through the summer . . . and so on by way of Michaelmas daisies, bright berries and the conflagration of autumn colours on the trees, to the clean, austere beauty of bare trunks and boughs.

Returning to an old thought—who can measure the beneficent influence exerted by this loveliest of gardens through the long years of its existence, and still continuing?

And now as we look back over the old gardens of London that we have visited, and remember the work done in them by faithful gardeners, and the pleasure taken in them by kings and commoners, churchmen, statesmen and "all sorts and conditions of men," the words of Sir William Temple, in his *Gardens of Epicurus*, come to mind: "The use of gardens . . . as it has been the inclination of Kings and the choice of Philosophers, so it has been the common favourite of public and private men; a pleasure of the greatest and the care of the meanest; and indeed an employment and a possession for which no man is too high or too low."

SELECT BIBLIOGRAPHY

The Story of the Garden.—Elinour Sinclair Rohde. (Medici Society, 1932.)

A History of Gardening in England.—Hon. Mrs. Evelyn Cecil. (John Murray, 1910.)

Herbs and Herb Gardening.—Elinour Sinclair Rohde. (Medici Society, 1936.)

A History of English Gardening.—George W. Johnson. (Baldwin & Cradock & Longman & Co., 1829.)

Gardens of Celebrities and Celebrated Gardens.—Jessie Macgregor. (Hutchinson & Co., 1918.)

Survey of London.—John Stow, 1633. (Kingsford.)

Old and New London.—(Various authors.) (Cassell, 1873–8.)

Early London.—Sir Walter Besant. (Adam & Charles Black, 1908.)

Mediaeval London.—Sir Walter Besant. (Adam & Charles Black, 1906.)

Survey of London North of the Thames.—Sir Walter Besant. (Adam & Charles Black, 1911.)

London Parks and Gardens.—Lady Evelyn Cecil. (Constable, 1907.)

Encyclopaedia of London.—Edited by William Kent. (J. M. Dent, 1937.)

Historical Memorials of Westminster Abbey.—Arthur Penrhyn Stanley. (John Murray, 1868.)

Westminster Abbey.—H. F. Westlake. (Philip Allan & Co., 1933.)

The Inns of Court and Chancery.—W. J. Loftie. (Seeley & Co., Ltd., 1895.)

A Short History of Lincoln's Inn.—Sir Gerald Hurst, K.C. (Constable, 1946.)

The Inner and Middle Temple.—Hugh H. L. Bellot, M.A., B.C.L. (Methuen, 1902.)

The Temple, London.—J. Bruce Williamson. (John Murray, 1924.)

A Calender of the Inner Temple Records.—Edited by F. A. Inderwick, 1896.

A Calender of the Middle Temple Records.—Edited by Charles Henry Hopwood, K.C., 1903.

Gray's Inn: Its History and Associations.—William Ralph Douthwaite. (Reeves & Turner, 1886.)

Gray's Inn (reprinted from *Country Life*, November 6th and 13th, 1937).

Bacon's Essays, 1612.

Charterhouse in London.—Gerald S. Davies. (John Murray, 1921.)

Syon House Trees and Shrubs.—A. Bruce Jackson. (West, Newman & Co., 1910.)

Henry VIII and the English Monasteries.—Cardinal F. A. Gasquet. (Geo. Bell & Sons, Ltd., 1925.)

The Catholic Encyclopaedia.—(New York, 1912.)

English Episcopal Palaces.—Edited by R. S. Raft. (Constable, 1910.)

The Story of Lambeth Palace.—Dorothy Gardiner. (Constable, 1930.)

The Diary of Samuel Pepys. (1659–69.)

The History of the Gardeners' Company.—Charles Welch, F.S.A. (London, 1900.)

London's Livery Companies.—Colonel Robert J. Blackham. (Sampson Low, Marston & Co., Ltd.)

The City Gardener.—Thomas Fairchild. (1722.)

The History of Hampton Court (3 vols.).—Ernest Law. (Geo. Bell & Sons, Ltd., 1888–91.)

A Short History of Hampton Court.—Ernest Law. (Geo. Bell & Sons, Ltd., 1924.)

The Gardens of Hampton Court.—Mollie Sands. (Evans Bros., Ltd., 1950.)

Dictionary of National Biography.

Parkinson's *Paradisus.* (1629.)

L.C.C. Survey of London, under the general editorship of Sir Lawrence Gomme & Philip Norman. Vol. IV, *Parish of Chelsea,* Part II. (Batsford, 1912.)

John Evelyn's Diary. (1641–97.)

Sir William Temple upon the Gardens of Epicurus with other 17th-century Garden Essays. (Chatto & Windus, 1908.)

The Royal Hospital, Chelsea.—C. G. T. Dean, M.B.E. (Hutchinson, 1950.)

The Romance of the Apothecaries' Garden at Chelsea.—F. D. Drewitt. (Chapman & Hall, 1922.)

Gleanings in Old Garden Literature.—W. Carew Hazlitt. (Elliott Stock, 1887.)

The Work of William Kent.—Margaret Jourdain. (Country Life, Ltd., 1948.)

The Environs of London, Vol. II.—Rev. Daniel Lysons (1795).

Bygone Richmond.—H. M. Cundell. (John Lane, 1925.)

Royal Gardens.—Cyril Ward. (Longmans Green & Co., 1912.)

The Story of Buckingham Palace.—Bruce Graeme. (Hutchinson & Co., Ltd.), 1928.

A Century of Buckingham Palace.—Bruce Graeme. (Hutchinson & Co., Ltd., 1937.)

Buckingham Palace, its Furniture, Decoration and History.—H. Clifford Smith. (Country Life, Ltd., 1931.)

The Royal Botanic Gardens, Kew.—W. J. Bean. (Cassell & Co., Ltd., 1908.)

The Romance of Kew.—Devised and edited by J. A. Jerome, B.A. Cantab. (Hampton Court Books, Molesey-on-Thames.)

INDEX

The numerals in **heavy type** refer to the *figure numbers* of illustrations.

INDEX